RIVER THAMES DOCKLAND HERITAGE

LONDON BRIDGE TO GREENWICH

MALCOLM BATTEN

AMBERLEY

First published 2022

Amberley Publishing
The Hill, Stroud
Gloucestershire, GL5 4EP

www.amberley-books.com

ISBN 978 1 3981 0876 9 (print)
ISBN 978 1 3981 0877 6 (ebook)

British Library Cataloguing in Publication Data.
A catalogue record for this book is available from the British Library.

Orgination by Amberley Publishing.
Printed in the UK.

Contents

Introduction

London owes its existence to the River Thames. Like many of the world's great cities, a navigable river meant trade, and with it came wealth. The site of the original Roman London was at the nearest point to the estuary where the tidal river was bridgeable with the technology available at the time. The original London Bridge then became the limit of navigation for any vessels that could not pass under it and so the wharves, warehouses, docks and all the other ancillary activities that facilitate port trade came to be accommodated to the east of the bridge. So important was the need for navigable access that no other bridge to the east of London Bridge was built until Tower bridge, with its opening bascule spans opened in 1894. Even since then, only one other bridge, the Queen Elizabeth II Bridge, opened at Dartford in 1991, has been built further down river.

London's docks grew in a piecemeal pattern. Originally there were the 'Legal Quays' at Billingsgate where all imported goods had to be delivered for inspection and assessment by customs officers. By the end of the eighteenth century the riverbank around the Tower of London was crowded with wharves and warehouses, while the tidal river was congested with shipping trying to reach them. Smuggling and theft were rife. The solution was to build enclosed docks with a permanent water level controlled by lock gates. The first commercial dock to be opened, by the West India Dock Company in 1802, was on the Isle of Dogs. Four years later a second dock was added, and the East India Dock Company opened its own dock at Blackwall. Others followed, for example London Docks (1805), St Katharine Dock (1828), Poplar Dock (1852), all on the north bank; and what were to become known as the Surrey Commercial Docks were developed from around the Howlands Great Dock on the south side. This had been the first enclosed dock, constructed back in 1696, but was used only for fitting out, ship repair and by the whaling fleet.

Victoria (later Royal Victoria) Dock opened further downriver in 1855. This was the first to be designed specifically for steamships and to have rail access. This was followed by Millwall Docks in 1868, Royal Albert Dock in 1880, and the first development at Tilbury, 22 nautical miles downriver in 1886.

The various docks were owned by a number of companies who competed not only with each other, but also with the private riverside wharves. They were losing money. So, following a Royal Commission report of 1902, a single unified port authority, the Port of

London Authority, was set up in 1909. In 1921 the 'Royal' group of docks was completed with the opening of the King George V (KGV) Dock by His Majesty on 8 July. Between them, the Royal Docks comprised the largest area of impounded dock water in the world, with over 11 miles of quays.

The Port of London reached its peak in terms of tonnage handled in 1964 when a total of 61,339,000 tons passed through the port. But changes in cargo handling methods, in particular the development of containerisation and Roll-on, Roll-off vehicle ferries, led to a drastic change to PLA policy. The existing docks were seen as unsuited to these new methods, and so it was decided that all future investment would be at downriver at Tilbury. The older docks would be closed. First to go were the East India Dock and Regent's Canal Dock in 1967. The latter was operated not by the Port of London Authority but by the British Waterways Board. In 1968 the PLA closed the St Katharine Docks and London Docks. These docks, closest to London, could only handle smaller vessels and were not rail connected. The Surrey Docks, on the south side of the river, followed in 1970. These specialised in timber traffic but as more of this became shipped on pallets rather than loose, the traffic transferred to other docks. The West India and Millwall Docks closed in 1980. General cargo ceased from the Royal Docks in 1981, with scrap metal business transferring to Tilbury in 1983. After that the docks were just used for laid-up shipping until the final vessels moved out in 1985.

It was not just the enclosed docks that were affected by these changes. There were the numerous private wharves and warehouses alongside the river and up the creeks off the Thames that were served by lighters under the 'Free Water clause'. These have also nearly all closed other than those specialising in aggregates, chemicals and domestic refuse traffic. There were coal or oil-fired power stations and gasworks that have also closed as energy supply has switched to renewables rather than polluting fossil fuels.

Accompanying the closure of the docks, the London Docklands Development Corporation was set up in 1981 to redevelop the West India and Millwall Docks sites and later the Royal Docks lands. This had powers to cut through some of the red tape normally associated with redevelopment. The Millwall and West India Docks became Docklands – the business and housing developments around Canary Wharf. The Royals are now home to London City Airport, the University of East London and the Excel Exhibition Centre.

Heritage was not forgotten, and there are many reminders of the past. St Katharine Dock was redeveloped as a marina. Various preserved vessels were offered moorings there, and although most of these have since moved on, the dock is still home for a selection of the former Thames sailing barges.

Dockyard offices and warehouses survive in alternative commercial use. Riverside wharf warehouses were converted to luxury apartments. Elsewhere disused bridges, cranes, hydraulic accumulator towers and capstans remain as reminders of what went on before. Informative plaques, statues and other artworks also commemorate the past. But the history of London's dockland past can best be appreciated by a visit to the Museum of London Docklands, part of the Museum of London and housed in one of the 1802-built Grade I listed warehouses in West India Dock.

In its working days, much of the riverbank was inaccessible to the general public. Tall security walls closed off the wharves and docks, and elsewhere gasworks, power stations and other industrial sites were equally closed off. The best way to appreciate the river was on one of the pleasure trips that ran from Tower Pier to Greenwich. Until the 1960s there were also trips that ran on to Woolwich and then into the Royal Docks to view the shipping within. Pleasure trips still run between Tower Pier and Greenwich, with some continuing to the Thames barrier. Additionally the commuter ferry services run by Thames Clippers link central London with Greenwich, with services at certain times continuing to the O2 Arena and Woolwich Arsenal Pier. A number of new piers have been constructed along the river as pick up/set down points for Thames Clippers.

The opening of the Thames Path from 1996 has opened up new vistas of the river. This runs along both sides of the river, following the riverbank wherever possible, and has opened up new opportunities for walkers, cyclists (in parts) and tourists.

This book follows the route of the Thames Path on each bank, starting at London Bridge and ends at Greenwich. On the way there will be detailed looks at each of the former dock networks on either side of the river to see how they have been redeveloped and what remains. Also included will be other infrastructure with maritime connections – including riverside private wharves, former power stations, and the bridges, tunnels and ferries that cross the river. The Regent's Canal network that distributed goods from the port around East London and onwards is included.

The sewer network designed by Sir Joseph Bazalgette in the 1860s ended the dumping of raw sewage directly into the river in central London, while continuing to use the river to dispose of the sewage at sea. This practice has now ended, and the sewer network is currently being upgraded by the multimillion-pound Thames Tideway 'Supersewer' to meet the needs of a much greater London population than that originally envisaged in the 1860s.

A few diversions will also look at other related items of interest.

A companion book will follow on to Woolwich, and then take the route of the Thames Path Extension to Erith. Finally, it will conclude with a look at Tilbury where the modern docks are situated, and on the opposite bank Gravesend, a town with a long maritime connection to London.

Beyond London Bridge

Although London Bridge was the limit of the port, this was (and still is not) the limit for commercial shipping. Ships may no longer transport coal to upriver power stations, but domestic rubbish is still transported downriver, and tugs with lighters and a few smaller coasters still bring aggregates to upriver wharves. Projects such as the Thames Tideway tunnel (or 'Supersewer') also generate river traffic. So, we will take a brief diversion to look at the river beyond London Bridge.

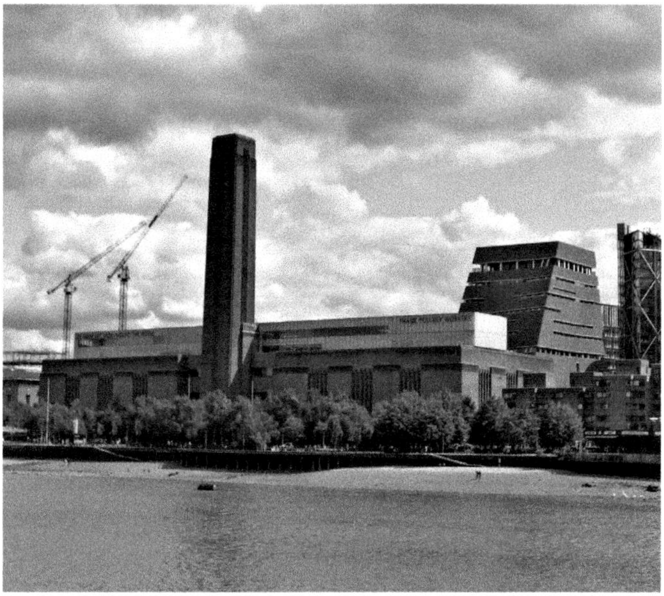

The former oil-fired Bankside 'B' Power Station designed by Sir Giles Gilbert Scott closed in 1981 and was converted to become the Tate Modern art gallery, which opened in May 2000. The Millennium footbridge, just off to the left, was opened in 2000 to connect the gallery to the north bank. The angled tower building is the extension, which opened in 2016.

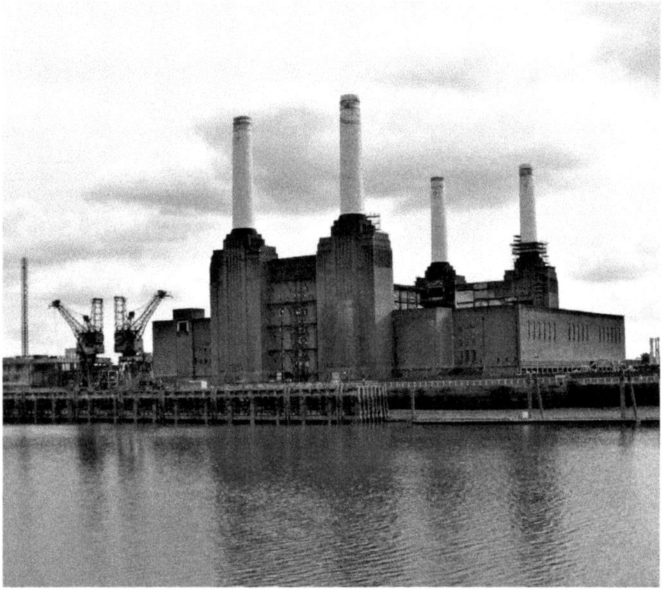

The most famous of London's riverside power stations is Battersea. Coal-fired Battersea Power Station was built in two stages – Battersea A between 1929 and 1935, and Battersea B between 1937 and 1955. At its peak it was providing one fifth of London's electricity. Closure came in 1975 for Battersea A and 1983 for Battersea B. Listed Grade II*, the site lay vacant for many years as various redevelopment plans fell by the wayside. The site was eventually purchased by Malaysian investors and redevelopment work started in 2014. This view is from 2013 before the redevelopment started.

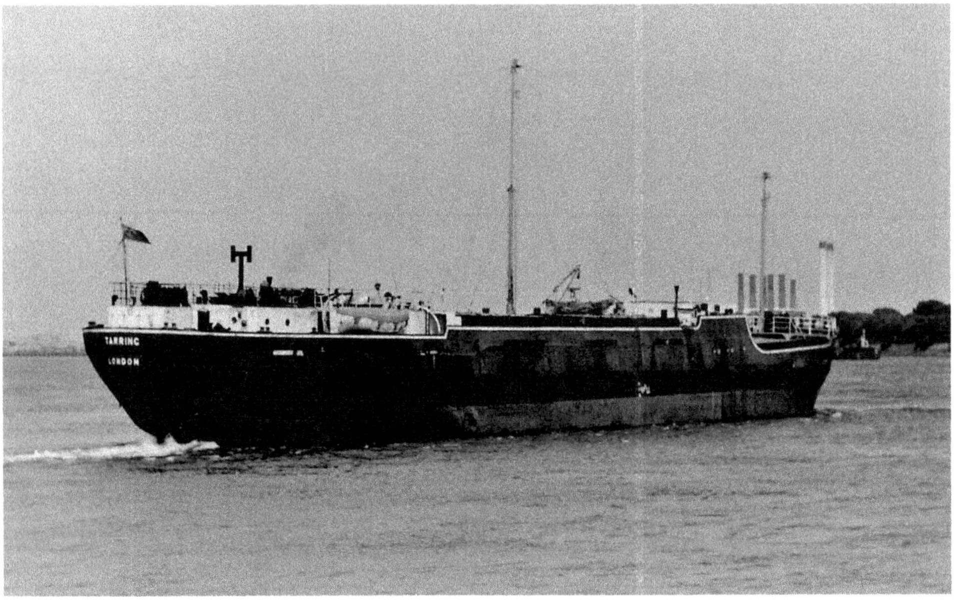

So-called 'flatirons' – colliers with a low superstructure to fit under the Thames bridges – would deliver to the upriver power stations such as Wandsworth and Battersea. This is the *Tarring* [London] of Stephenson Clarke passing Woolwich in 1977. (Reg Batten)

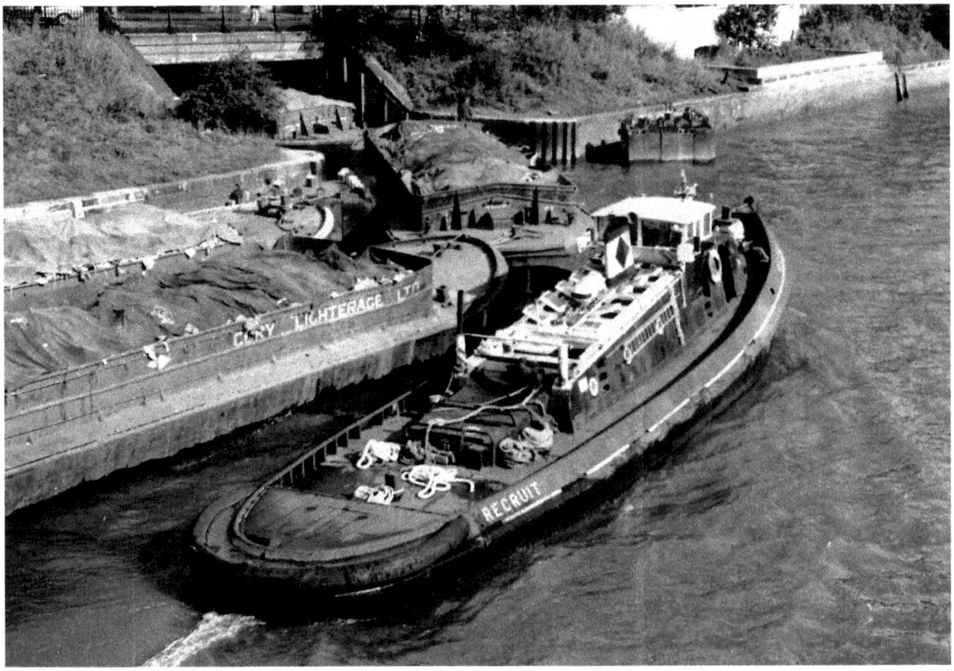

Until 1985 domestic rubbish for landfill was put into lighters and covered by a tarpaulin. Cory Lighterage Ltd tug *Recruit* marshalls lighters at the Gatliff Road wharf of Westminster City Council, close to Chelsea Bridge on 10 October 1977. From 1985 the refuse was containerised and transported in new purpose-built barges.

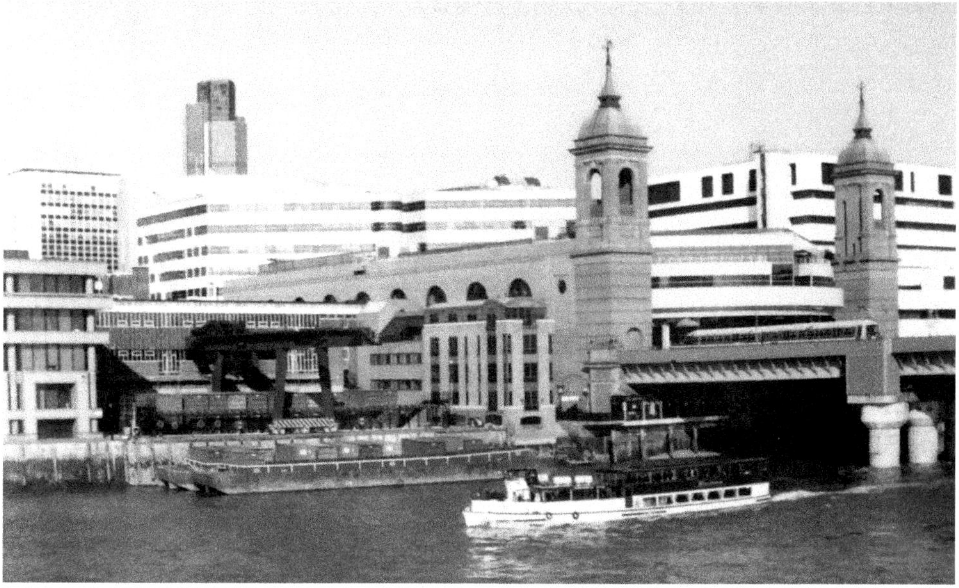

The City of London has a loading wharf alongside Cannon Street station, where a lighter is seen in 2000. In 1979 Cory Waste Management (now Cory Environmental) were given the contract by the Greater London Council to take containerised domestic rubbish from various loading points along the Thames to landfill sites at Rainham and Mucking or, nowadays, for incineration. In 2002 they were awarded a thirty-year contract to carry waste from the Western Riverside Waste Authority – the London boroughs of Hammersmith & Fulham, Lambeth and Wandsworth, and the Royal borough of Kensington & Chelsea. This now goes to the Riverside Resource Recovery Facility at Belvedere, which opened in 2011.

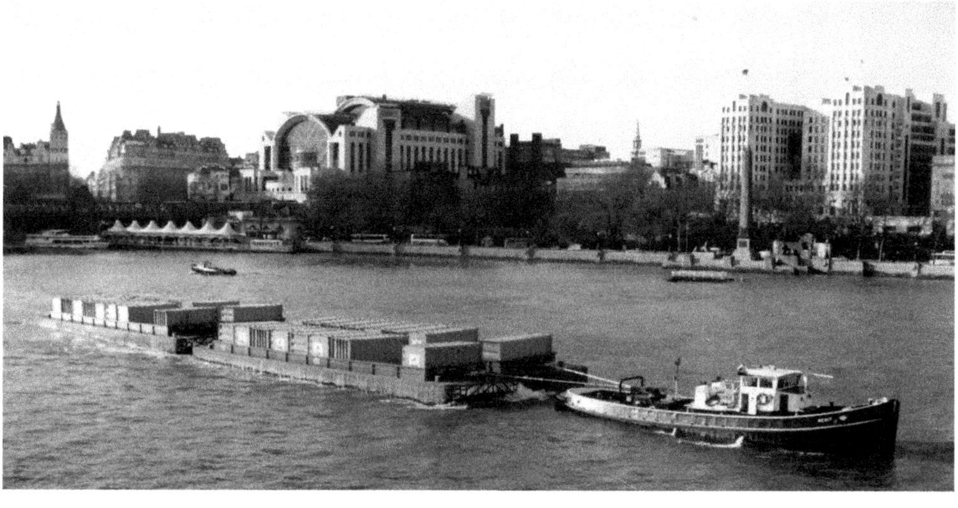

Victoria Embankment seen from Waterloo Bridge in January 1994. This was built in 1862 by Sir Joseph Bazalgette to carry the sewers and the District Railway. Tug *Merit* is towing containerised rubbish lighters downriver. The Cleopatra's Needle obelisk can be seen on the north bank. Hungerford Bridge is on the left carrying the railway to Charing Cross station, now surmounted by the large development seen.

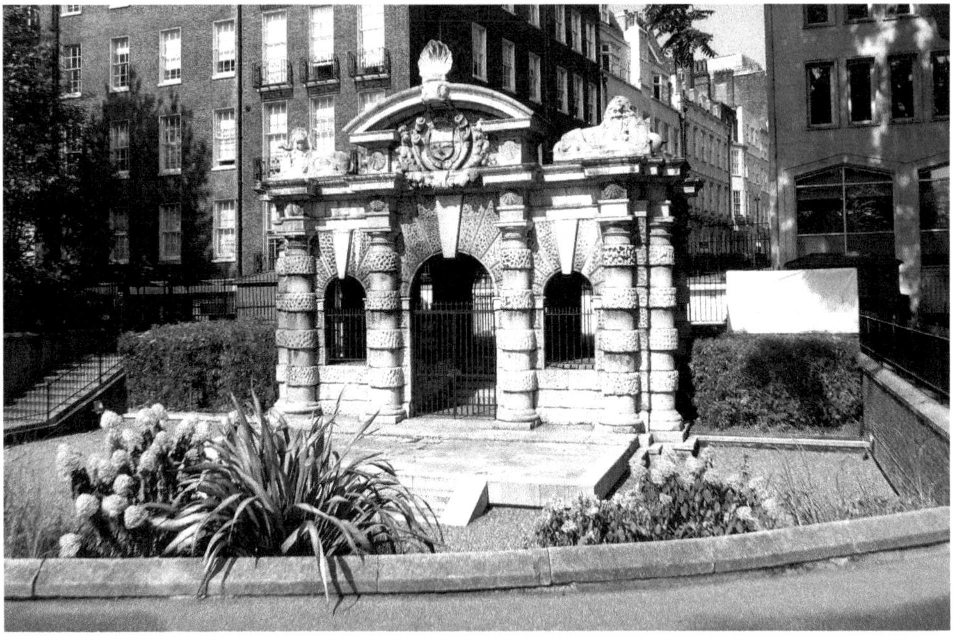

A large amount of land was reclaimed by the construction of the Victoria Embankment. The Embankment Gardens is built on part of this reclaimed land and the Watergate is a visible reminder of where the river used to reach before this project was begun.

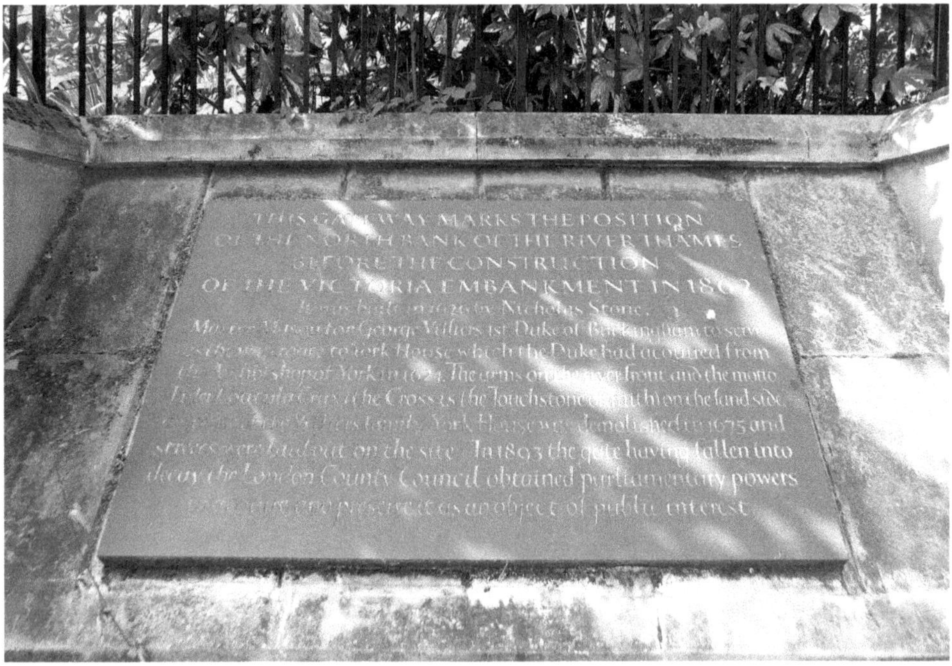

The Watergate plaque. The first part of the inscription reads 'This gateway marks the position of the north bank of the River Thames before the construction of the Victoria Embankment in 1862'.

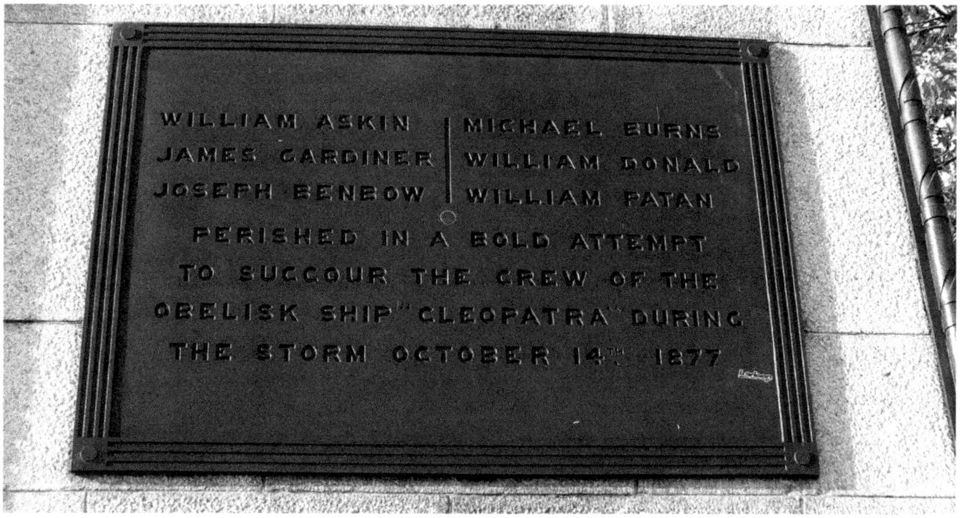

Cleopatra's Needle is the popular name given to the Egyptian obelisk erected on Victoria Embankment, although this dates from *c.* 1450 BC, about a thousand years before her reign. Formerly in Alexandria, it was presented to Britain in 1819 but not shipped over until 1877. A special pontoon, the *Cleopatra*, was built at Thames Iron Works to contain the obelisk as it was towed to Britain. A fierce storm led to the *Cleopatra* losing control and six men were drowned in an attempt to rescue her. This plaque commemorates their bravery. On arrival in 1878 four Tangye hydraulic pumps, each worked by one man, were used to erect the Needle.

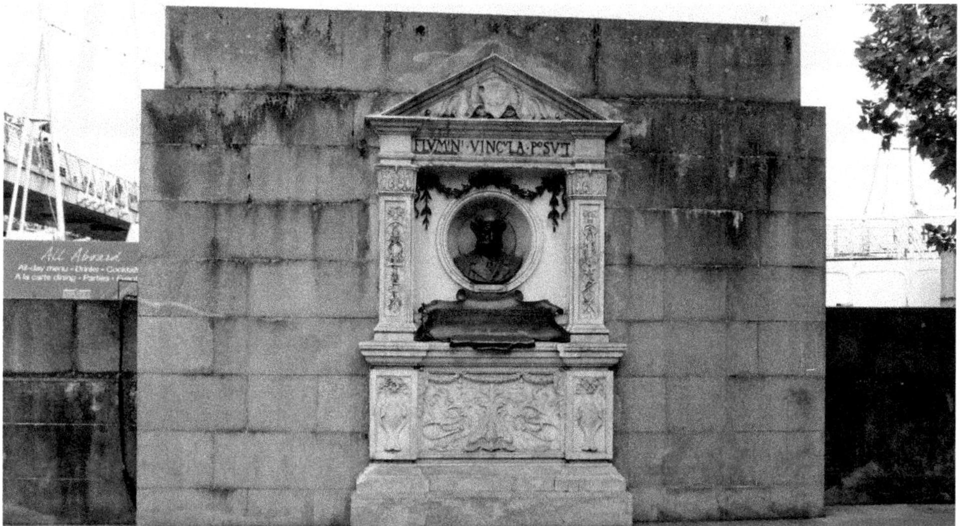

Just west of Hungerford Bridge on the Victoria Embankment is this memorial to its builder Sir Joseph Bazalgette. Born in March 1819, he was Chief Engineer to the Metropolitan Board of Works from 1856. Following major outbreaks of cholera culminating in the 'Great Stink' of 1858, Parliament passed an Act allowing the construction of a sewer network for London. It was thought at the time that cholera was caused by 'miasma – the stink of foul air from raw sewage – and that burying the sewage in sewers would eliminate this. In fact, cholera was caused from contaminated water, but the sewers succeeded by removing the bacteria.

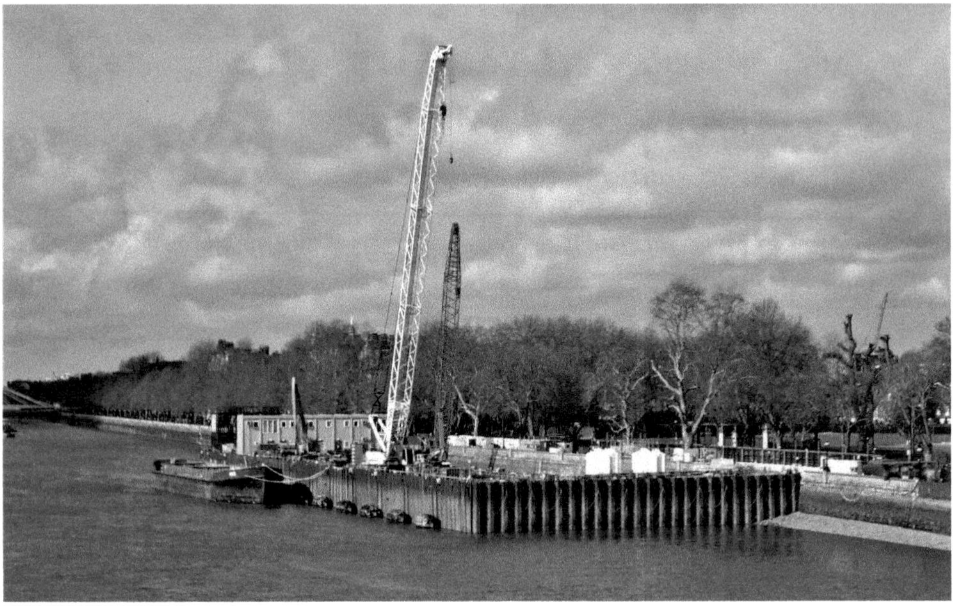

A pusher tug propels a lighter loaded with spoil downriver, seen from Waterloo Bridge in 2019. It has possibly come from a Thames Tideway Supersewer construction site. Another Thames Tideway site can be seen by Blackfriars Bridge. St Paul's Cathedral still dominates the skyline despite the modern office blocks.

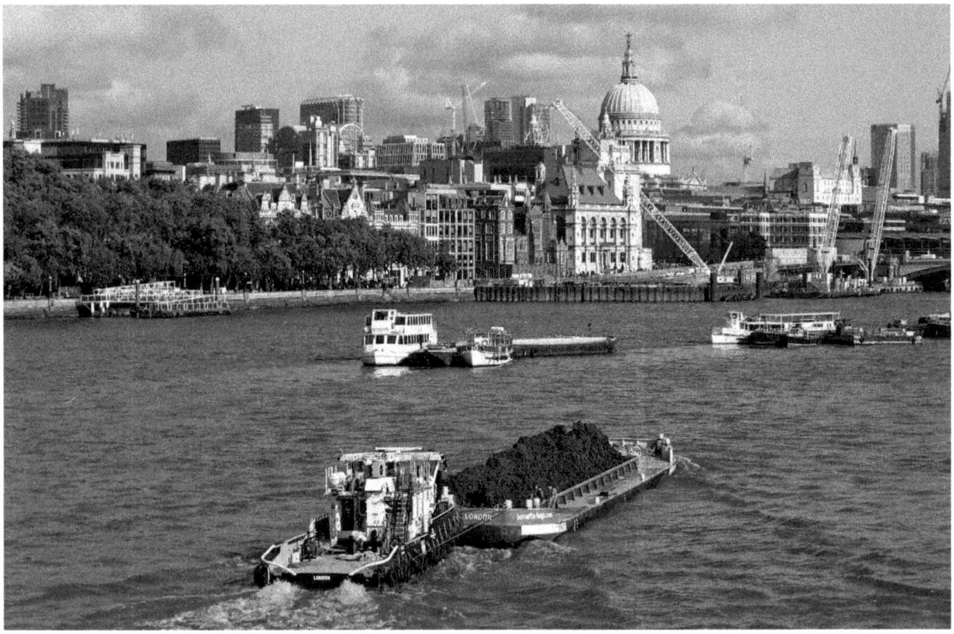

The Chelsea Embankment foreshore site of the Thames Tideway Supersewer works. A 50-metre-deep shaft is being built to intercept the current combined sewer overflows (CSOs) outside the Royal Hospital Chelsea and take that flow down into the new sewer below the river. This will also create a new area of public space by the river. April 2020.

The Upper Pool

The Upper Pool is the name given to the area between London Bridge and Tower Bridge. This was the original port before the enclosed docks were built and along with the Lower Pool (the area from Tower Bridge to Rotherhithe) was used by commercial shipping until the 1960s.

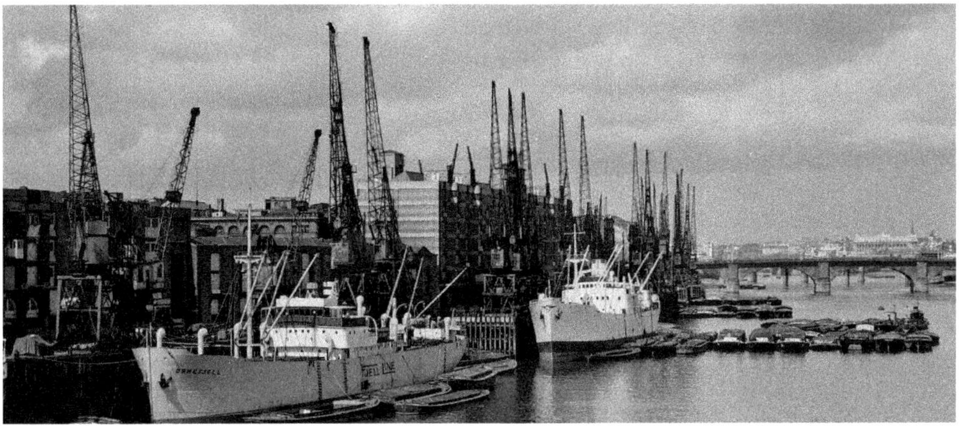

The south bank of the Upper Pool was full of commercial shipping wharves until the 1960s. This view from Tower Bridge in 1949 shows Fjell Line's *Ornefjell* in the foreground. Note the profusion of lighters for transhipment of goods to the various private wharves along the river and canal system. (Reg Batten)

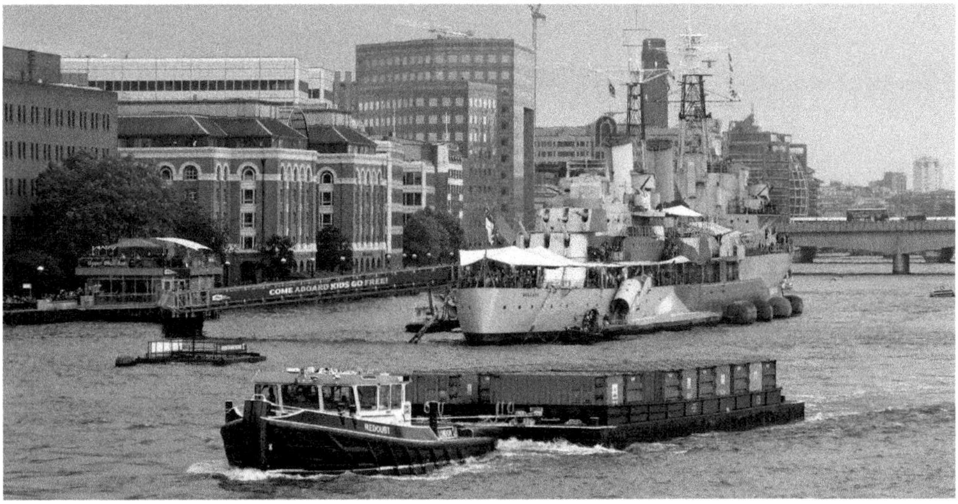

A similar view from Tower Bridge in 2014 with HMS *Belfast* prominent. Behind the access to this is the former Hays Wharf, now the Hays Galleria shopping centre. The Cory tug *Redoubt* heads downriver with a lighter laden with containerised rubbish. London Bridge in the distance has changed – the current bridge was built between 1967 and 1973 and is a box girder bridge made from concrete and steel. The exterior granite blocks of the previous 1830s bridge were removed and used to clad a new bridge in Lake Havasu City, Arizona.

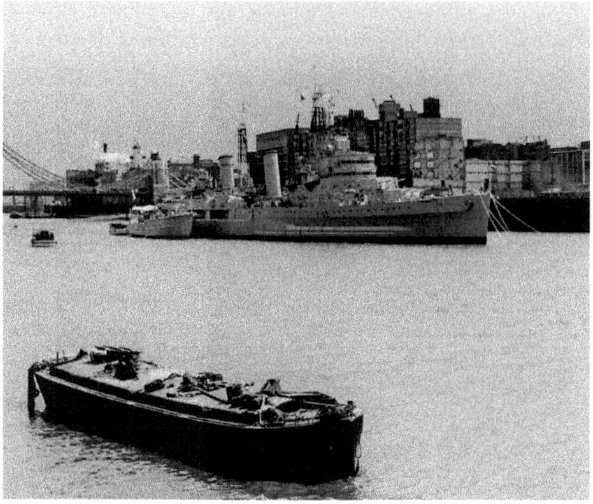

HMS *Belfast* was launched in 1938, and after twenty-five years of active service, she was retired in 1963. She was acquired by a trust on behalf of the Imperial War Museum and brought to London, opening to the public in October 1971. This 1970s view from London Bridge shows some of the former wharves being demolished. (Reg Batten)

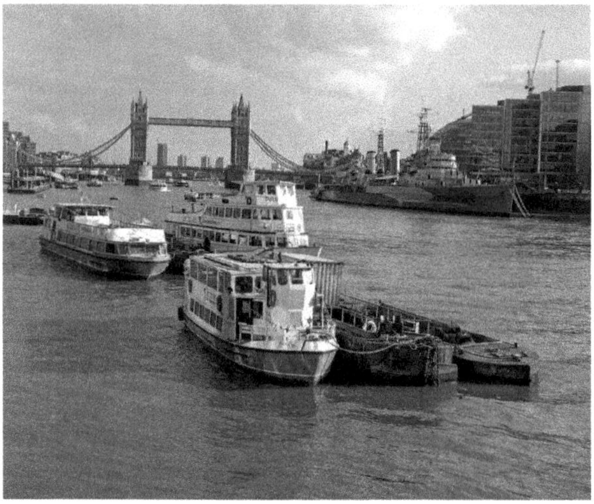

A more recent view showing some of the buildings that have replaced them on the south bank. These include the London City Hall building. The area is marketed as London Bridge City.

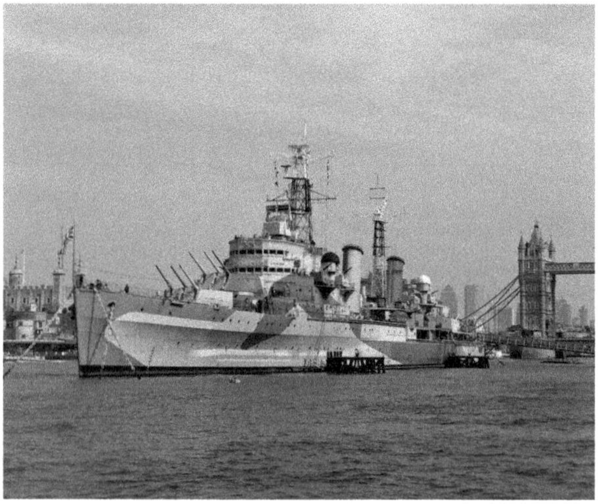

HMS *Belfast* is the only surviving British naval ship from the bombardment force that supported the D-Day Normandy landings on 6 June 1944, where she fired over 5,000 shells to assist the troops landing at Gold and Juno beaches. She was given a repaint in camouflage style during 1993. The new style is seen in 2019. The Tower of London on the north bank can be seen above her bows.

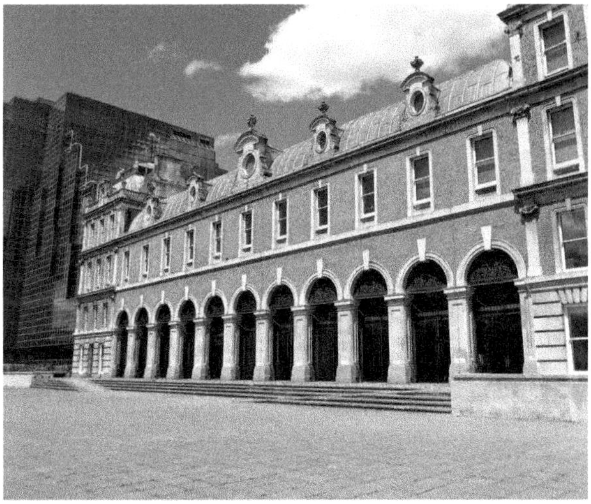

The old Billingsgate fish market is a fine Italianate structure dating from 1875, with an arcaded market hall. This was the main wholesale market for fish until 1982 when the market moved to a new site in Docklands.

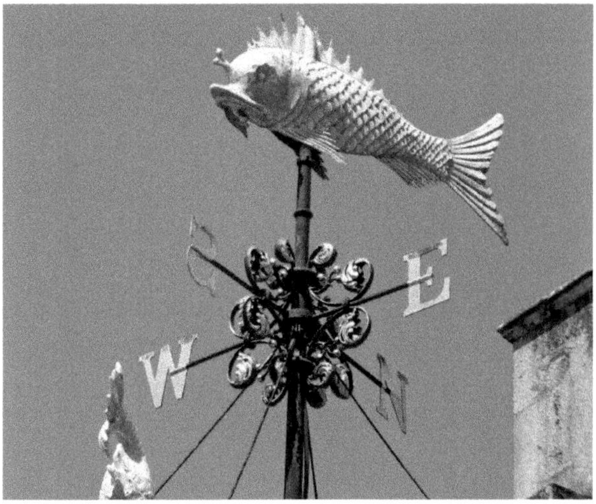

The old Billingsgate fish market is topped at each end with these appropriate weathervanes.

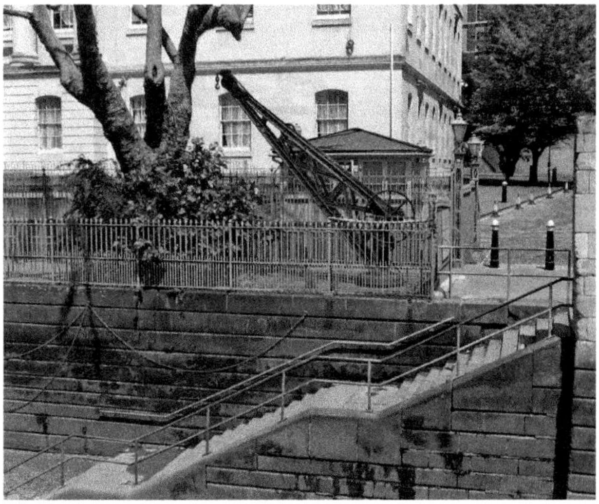

A small hand crane on the walkway in front of the former nineteenth-century Custom House building. There has been a Custom House here since at least the fourteenth century and until the enclosed docks were built any cargo arriving from overseas had to be assessed here. By the eighteenth century the river had become so congested with ships and pilfering was so rife that the enclosed docks came to be built.

NORTH BANK – LONDON BRIDGE TO ISLAND GARDENS

London Bridge – Tower Bridge

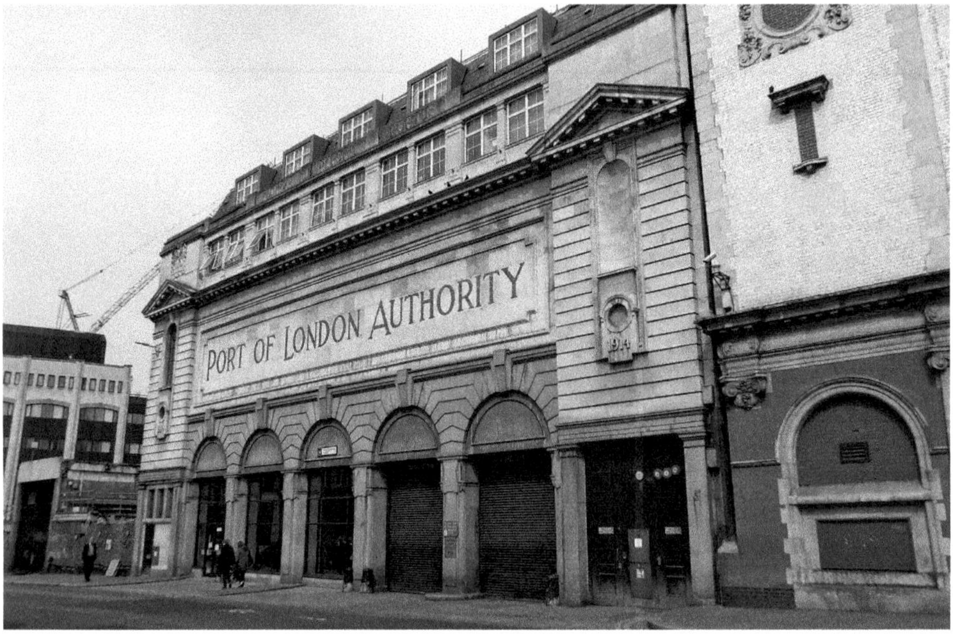

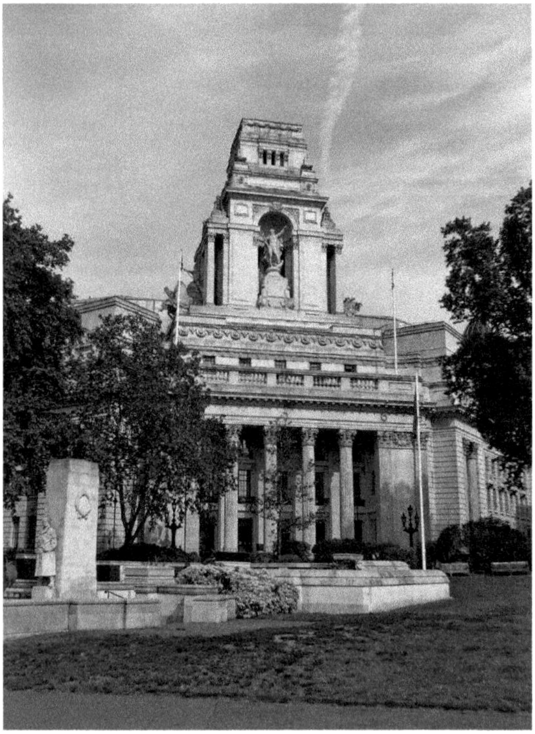

Above: The former Port of London Authority cold store in Charterhouse Street, Smithfield. This street contains several former refrigerated stores serving the meat market, also including the Central Cold Store and Metropolitan Cold Stores. The PLA cold store now houses a heat and power plant operated by Citigen.

Left: The PLA former headquarters building at Tower Hill, known as the 'Wedding Cake', opened in 1922. It was sold to an insurance firm in June 1972, being considered too large and expensive by this time of decline.

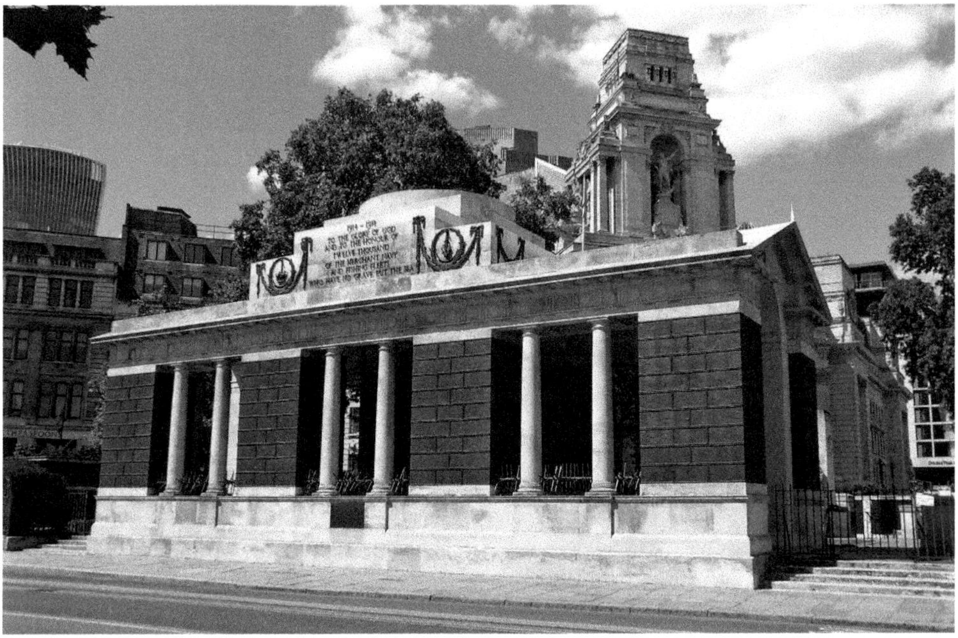

Above: The Merchantile Marine war memorial in Trinity Square Gardens, Tower Hill. This commemorates merchant seaman and fishermen who were killed as a result of enemy action in the First World War and have no known grave. Listed Grade I, it was designed by Sir Edward Lutyens and unveiled in 1928. The walls are clad with bronze panels listing the names of the missing. Behind it is the Merchant Seamans Memorial of 1955, commemorating the losses in the Second World War, and a memorial to losses in the Falklands War.

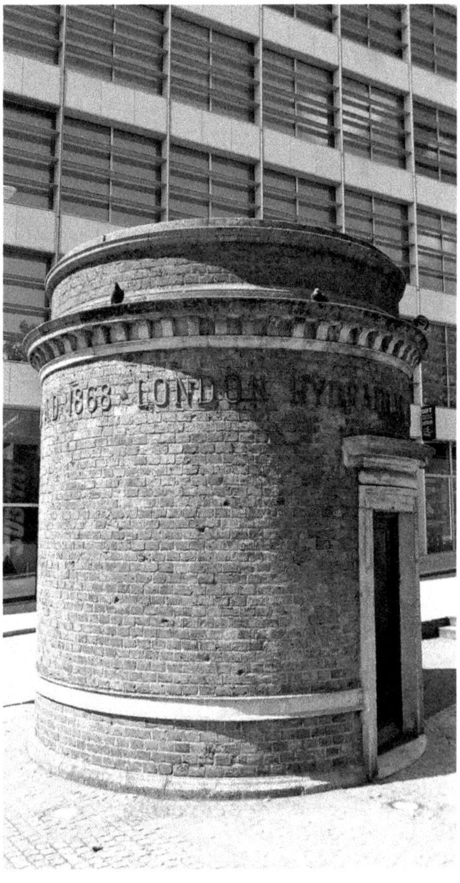

Right: The Tower Subway, a tunnel built in 1870 from Tower Hill to Vine Lane on the south side. It was built by Henry Greathead using his revolutionary tunnelling shield and was only the second tunnel bored under the river (the first was by Marc Brunel and now conveys the London Overground line). The 1,340-foot-long Thames tunnel originally carried a twelve-passenger cable car, but this proved unviable and it became a walkway. The opening of Tower Bridge in 1894 made it superfluous and it closed, being purchased by the London Hydraulic Power Co. to carry their mains. It thus became the only privately owned tunnel under the Thames. It now carries water mains for Thames Water.

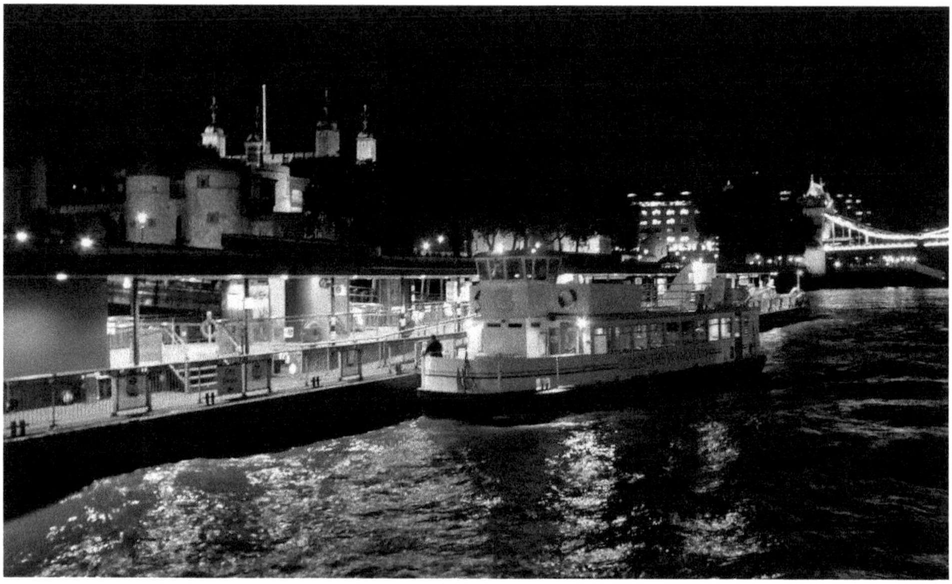

A night-time view of the Tower Millennium Pier by the Tower of London. This is the starting point for many of the tourist excursion craft that run down the river to Greenwich. In the evenings there are also party and dining trips on the river. Until the 1960s the Port of London Authority used to run excursions from here to the Royal Docks, entering the docks by the lock in Gallions Reach to view the ships inside. It was also the start point for paddle steamers to Southend and beyond, until these excursions stopped at the end of the 1966 season.

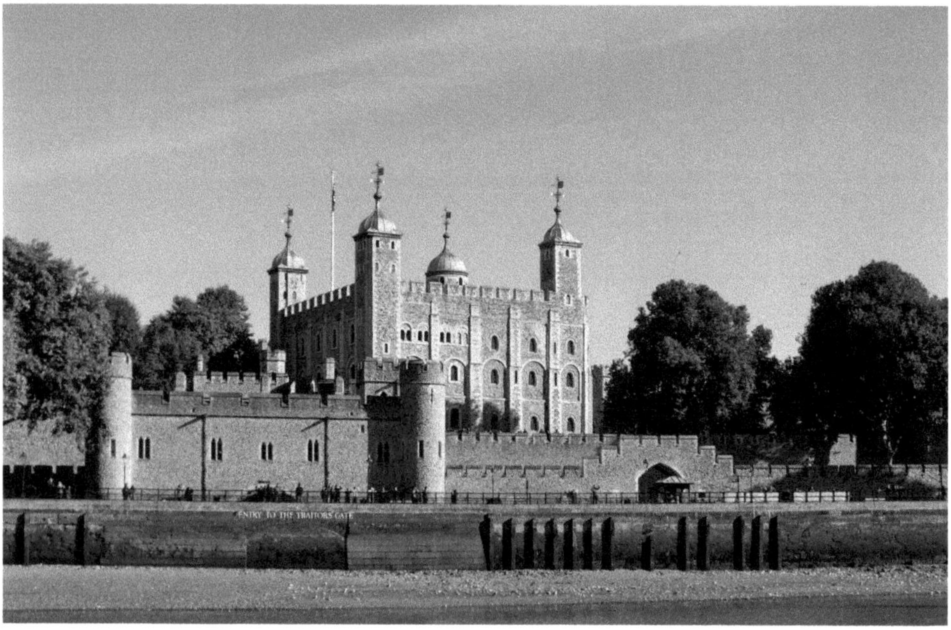

The Tower of London was built at the orders of King William I from *c.* 1078 onwards. The Traitors Gate river entrance at the base of St Thomas's Tower is so called because it was through here that those people accused of betraying the king or queen would be brought to be imprisoned.

Tower Bridge

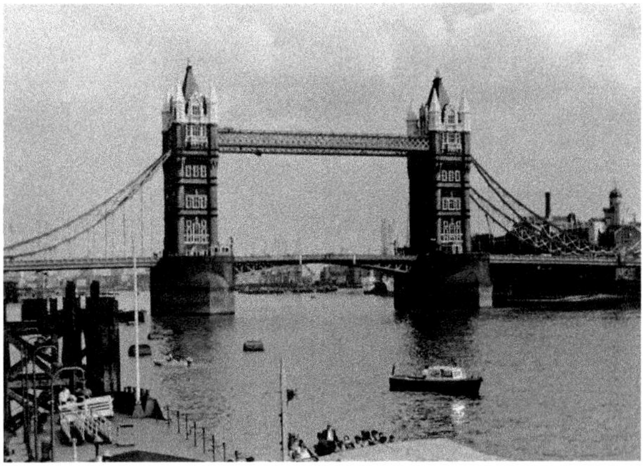

A view of Tower Bridge in the 1950s when both the Upper Pool and Lower Pool were busy with commercial shipping. Tower Bridge would be opened many times a day for shipping and a tug was kept on standby to assist if any ship got into difficulty passing through. Part of Tower Pier (now Tower Millennium Pier) is in the foreground. (Reg Batten)

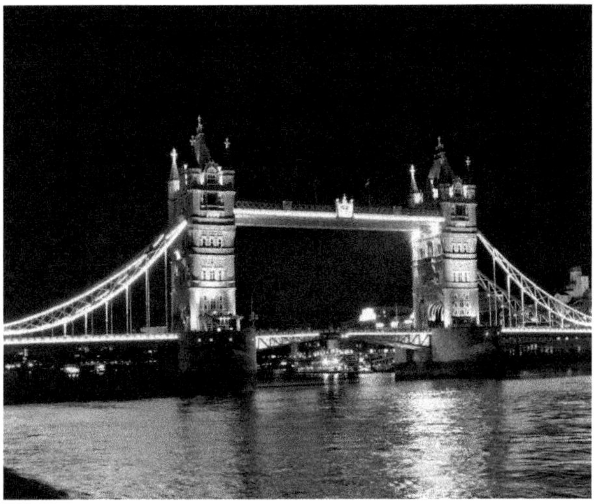

A view from roughly the same location in 2017. Tower Bridge is illuminated at night. Designed by Horace Jones, architect to the City of London, and John Wolfe Barry (both later knighted), construction started in 1886 and the bridge opened on 30 June 1894. The construction was masterminded by Sir William Arrol. The specification required an opening span of 200 feet and a headroom for ships of 135 feet. Each bascule with its counterweight inside the towers weighs some 1,045 tons. Tourists can now ascend inside the towers and traverse an upper walkway between the towers, as regular pedestrians had been able to until 1910.

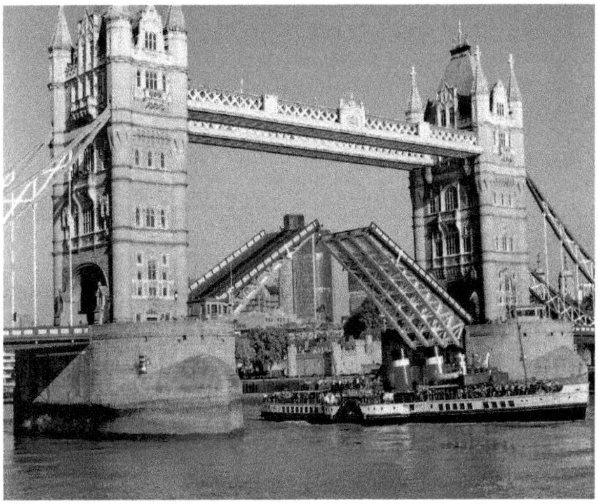

The world's last sea-going paddle steamer, the preserved 1947-built *Waverley,* passes under the bascules of Tower Bridge, which need to be raised to give clearance. *Waverley* is a popular visitor to the Thames on her annual programme of visits, running excursions to the likes of Southend, Clacton and Whitstable. Since the withdrawal of Eagle Steamers sailings at the end of the 1966 season there has been little opportunity to sail down the river beyond Woolwich, except on *Waverley.*

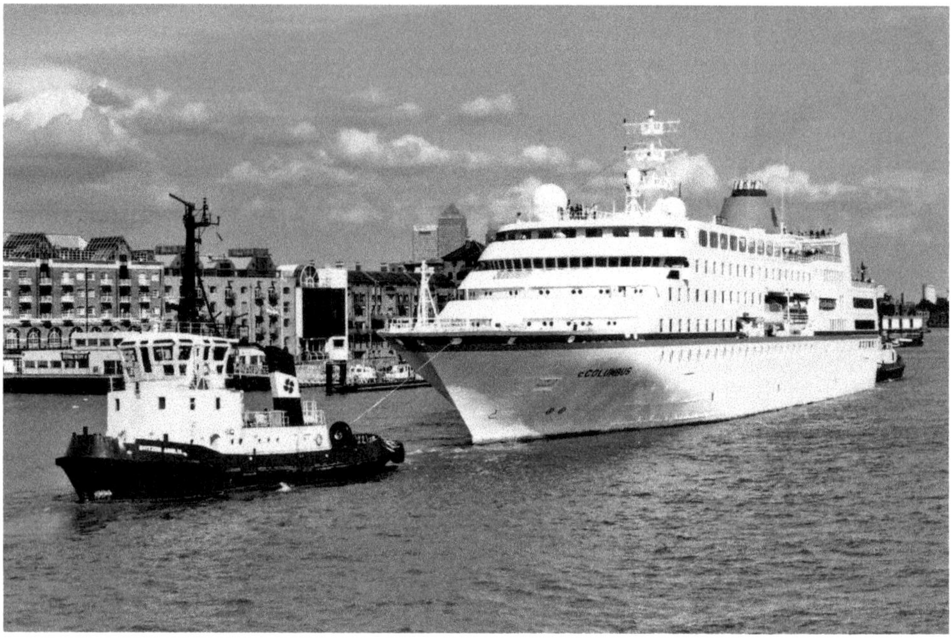

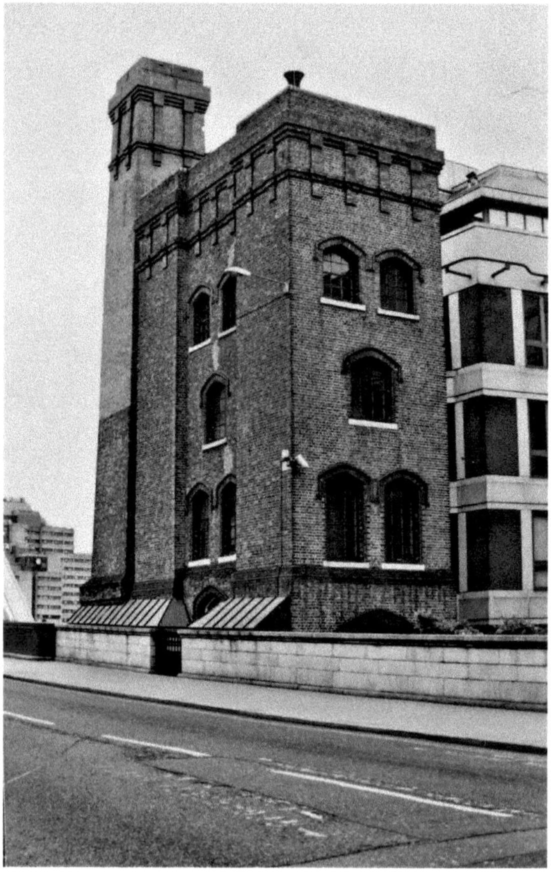

Above: From time to time cruise ships and naval or other vessels on courtesy visits will come up the Thames and berth alongside HMS *Belfast*, requiring a bridge lift. On 17 May 2010 the *C. Columbus* [Nassau] has been towed backwards through the bridge. She will then be turned by the tugs in the Lower Pool for her journey back down river. The times of arrival and departure and hence bridge lifts are governed entirely by the tides and not convenience to road traffic – a lift during the peak hour will cause disruption for some twenty minutes. Then there will be a second lift before or afterwards for the tugs fetching the ship or returning after berthing it.

Left: The bascules of Tower Bridge are raised hydraulically. Now the pumps are driven by electricity, but until 1976 this was by steam. The engine house and accumulator tower are on the south-east corner of the bridge. Parts of the original equipment can be seen as part of the 'Tower Bridge Experience'.

St Katharine Dock

St Katharine Dock was opened in 1828. Designed by Thomas Telford, it took the form of two linked basins with a common entrance lock. The warehouses designed by architect Philip Hardwick came right up to the quayside. The dock suffered badly in the Second World War, with all the warehouses around the eastern basin being destroyed. The dock could only handle smaller vessels and was one of the first to close in 1968. It was then sold to the Greater London Council and leased to developers Taylor Woodrow. The dock became a marina while new buildings including the World Trade Centre were built to create a successful regeneration.

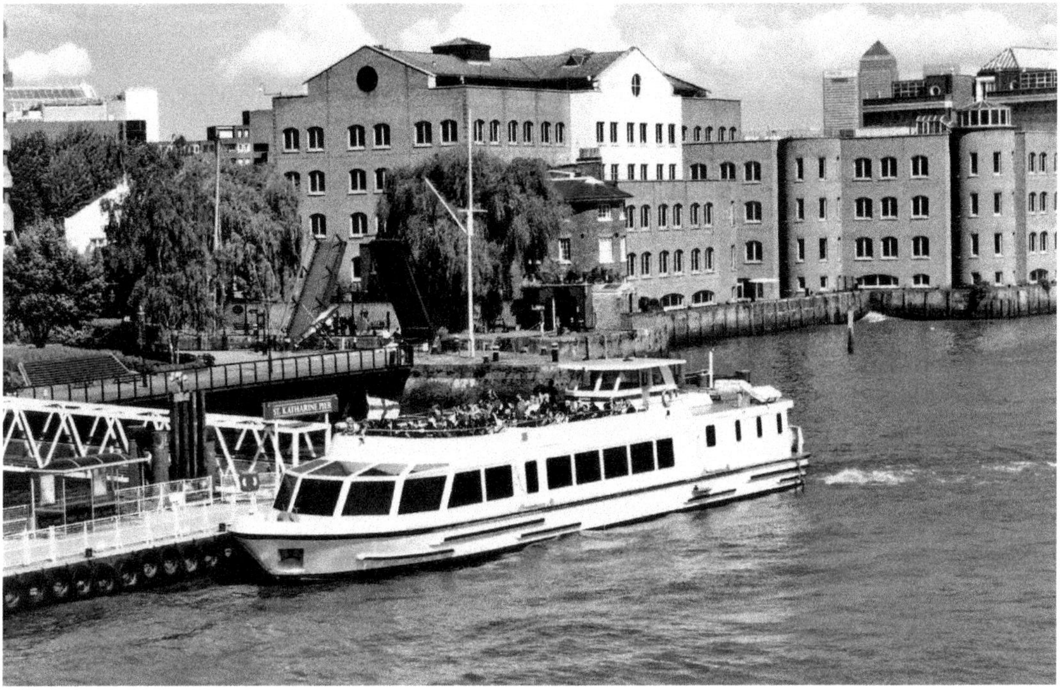

Immediately to the east of Tower Bridge is St Katharine Pier. In this view taken from the bridge one of the vessels of Crown River Cruises is on the pier. The Guoman Tower Hotel lies out of sight by the landward end of the pier. Beyond is the entrance to St Katharine Dock. The lock drawbridge to this is up – just visible between the trees.

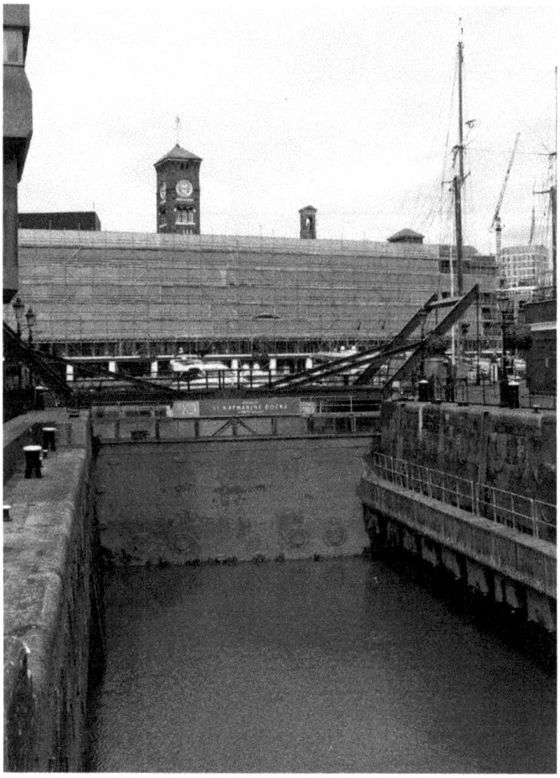

Left: The entrance lock to St Katharine Dock. The warehouses beyond were undergoing renovations in this view from 2020.

Below: On an earlier occasion the surviving original warehouses are seen in all their splendour. Although not the first enclosed dock to be built, this was the nearest to the City of London and the smallest.

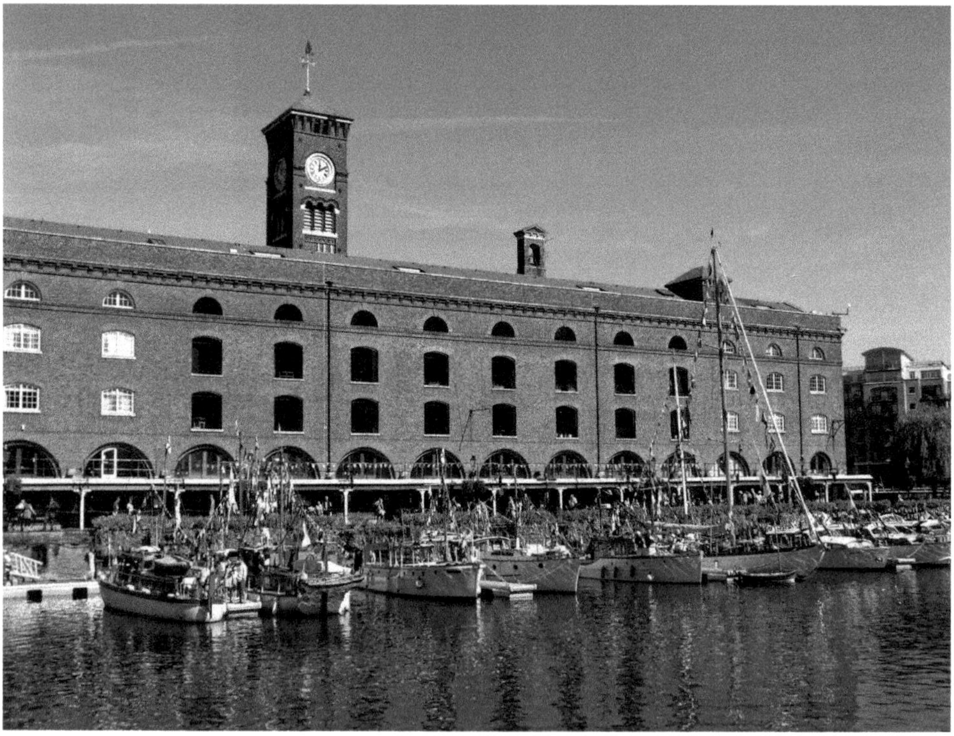

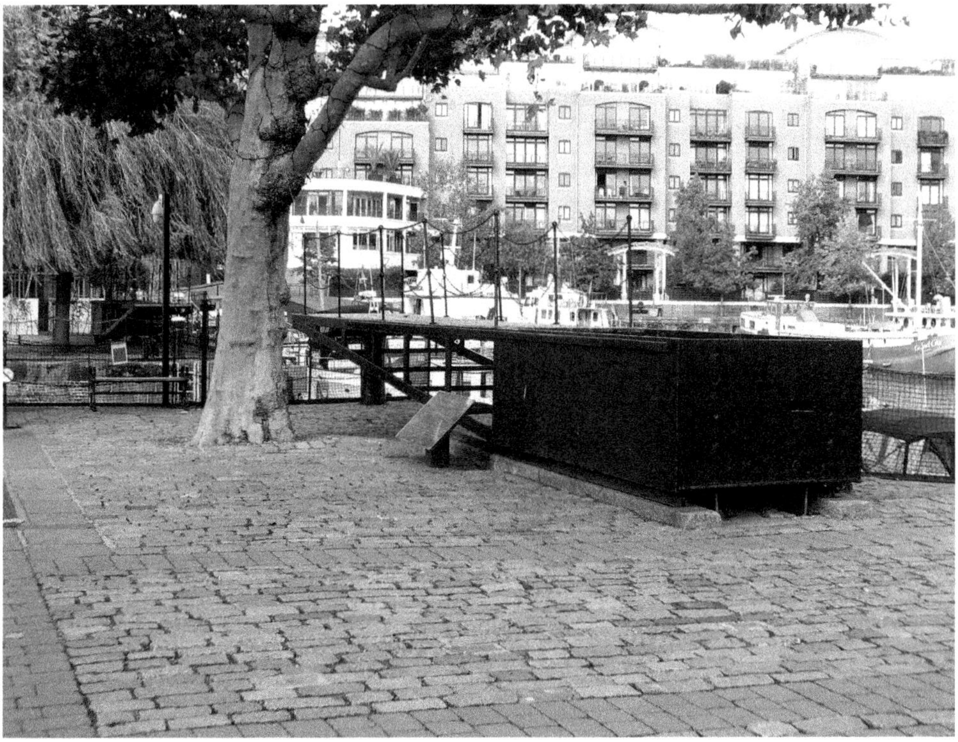

Above: Preserved within the dock is the Telford footbridge. This originally spanned the entrance to the East Dock until 1994. To allow entry to ships, the two halves of the wrought iron footbridge were withdrawn into recesses within the masonry on rails. The earliest plans for the bridge were signed by Thomas Rhodes, Thomas Telford's senior engineer.

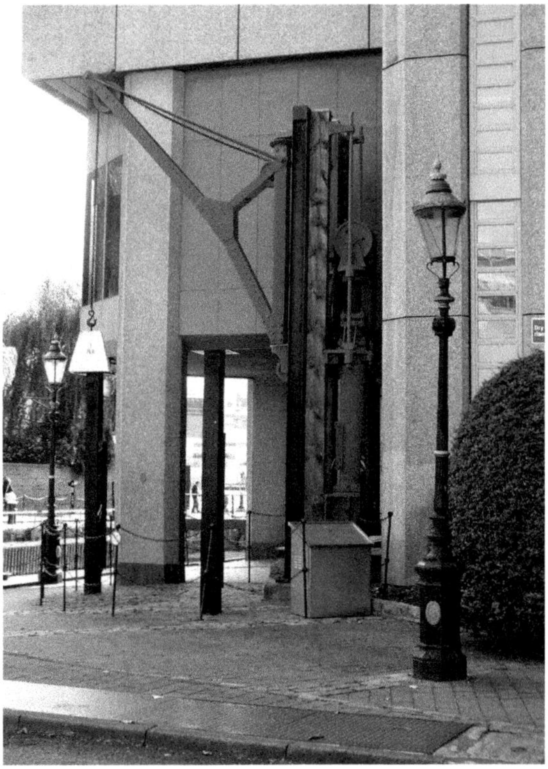

Right: At St Katharine Dock the warehouses were built right up to the quayside leaving no space for quayside cranes, so wall cranes were attached to the warehouses and hydraulic jiggers were fitted to operate them. Made by Armstrong's of Newcastle, these were introduced in the 1860s, falling out of use by the 1920s. An example of one of the cranes is preserved, attached to the wall of the Guoman Tower Hotel.

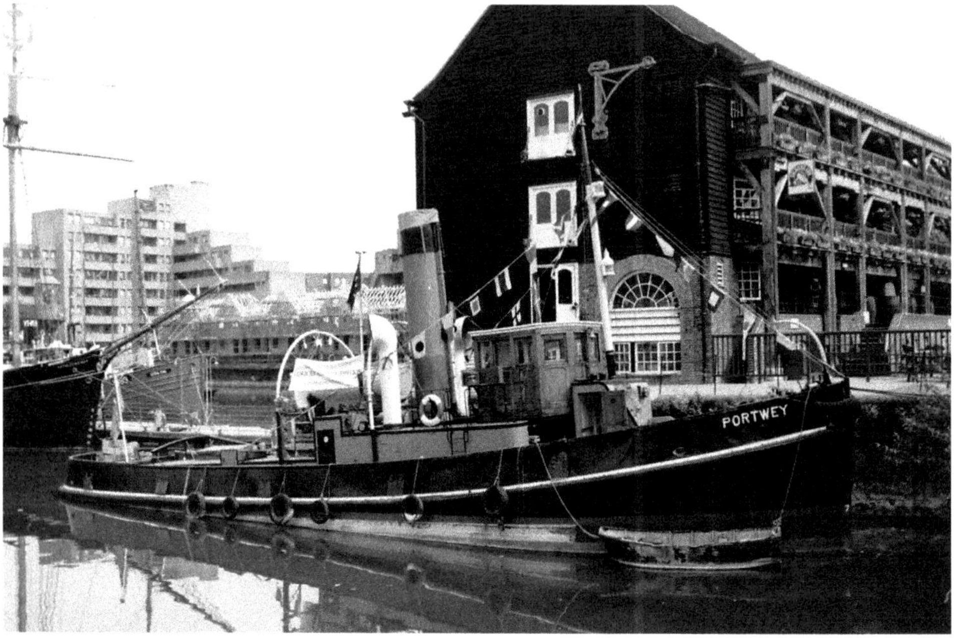

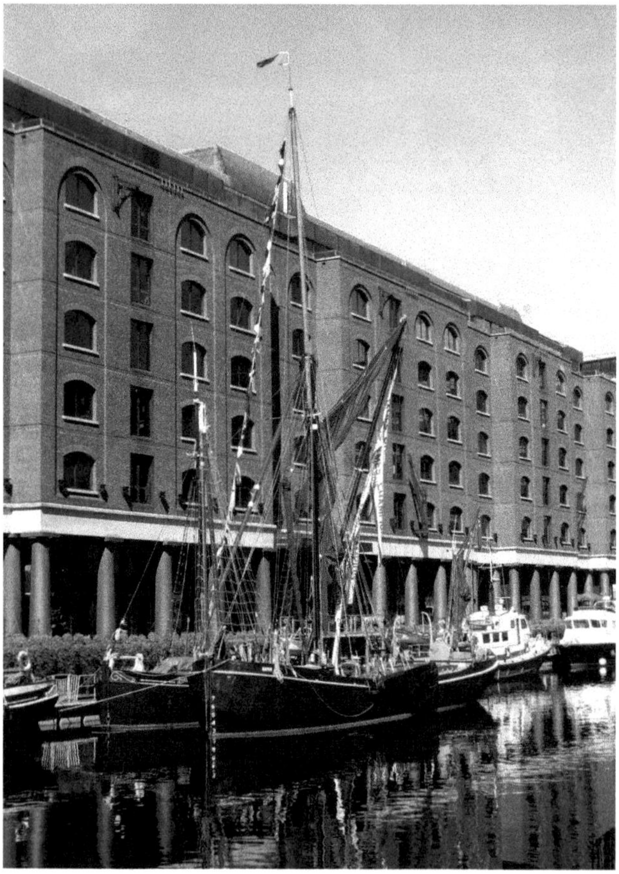

Above: The Maritime Trust, founded in 1969, had acquired a number of historic craft and were invited to display some of their collection in the marina. The Trust's collection was dispersed after 1986. In this view the tug *Portwey* takes centre stage. *Portwey* was owned by the Falmouth Docks & Engineering Co. Ltd and was built in 1927. She was sold for preservation in 1967 and donated to the Maritime Trust in 1982. Behind, the bows of *Discovery* (before she moved to Dundee) and *Lydia Eva* can be seen. (Reg Batten)

Left: Although the preserved vessels have since moved on, a selection of Thames barges can usually be seen within the marina. The buildings behind are modern, but designed to complement the original warehouses.

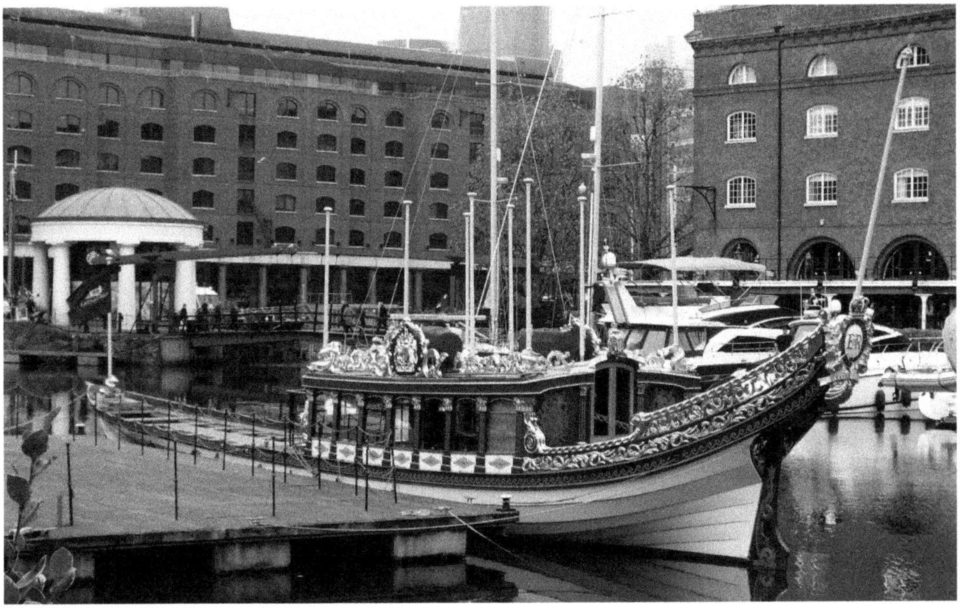

Royal rowing barge *Gloriana* in St Katharine Dock in 2014. She was privately commissioned and built for the Thames Diamond Jubilee Pageant of June 2012. She is 90 feet long and powered by eighteen oarsmen. The design was inspired by barges in Canaletto's eighteenth-century London paintings.

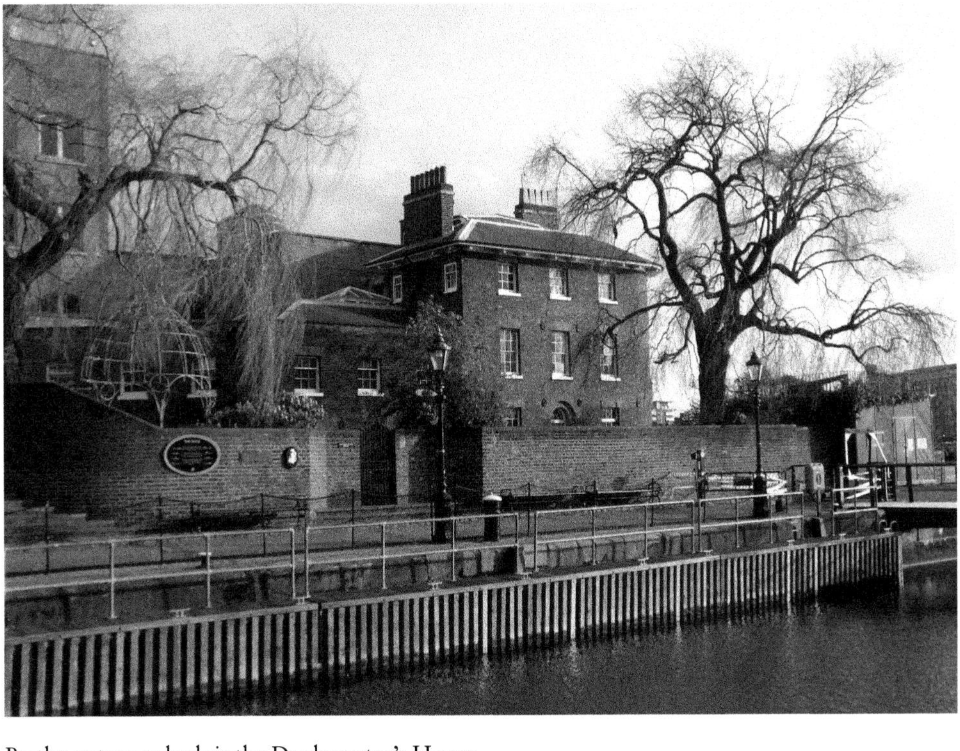

By the entrance lock is the Dockmaster's House.

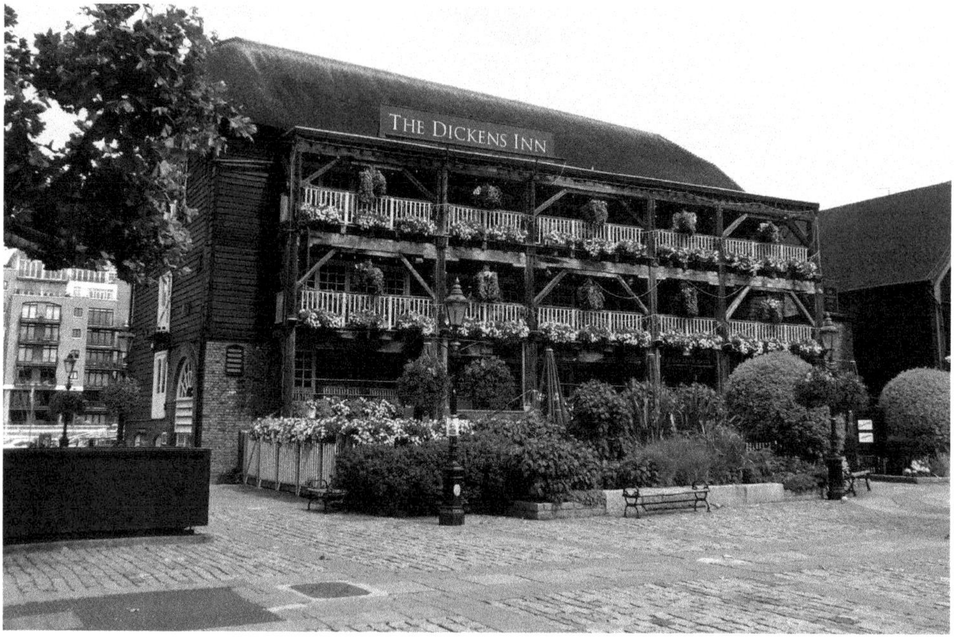

The Dickens Inn lies within the St Katharine Dock complex. Originally built in the eighteenth century, it was scheduled for demolition and redevelopment in the 1970s. However, instead it was moved 75 yards west to the position it occupies today.

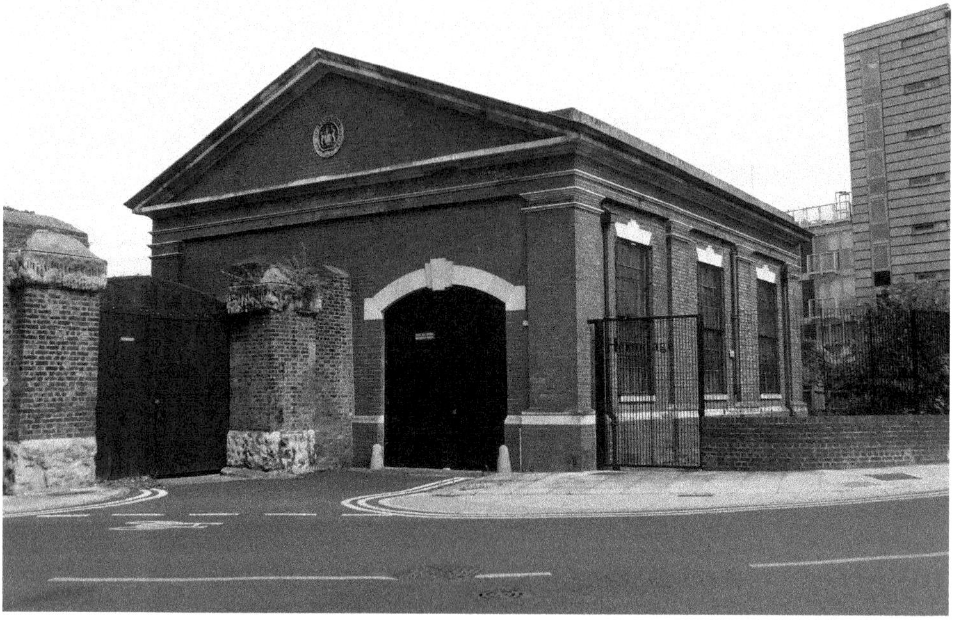

On the south-east corner of St Katharine Dock is this rather anonymous building with a PLA emblem. Its purpose is unclear, but buildings in a similar architectural style survive elsewhere in the former docks and they may have contained equipment to regulate the water level within the docks.

St Katharine Dock to Wapping

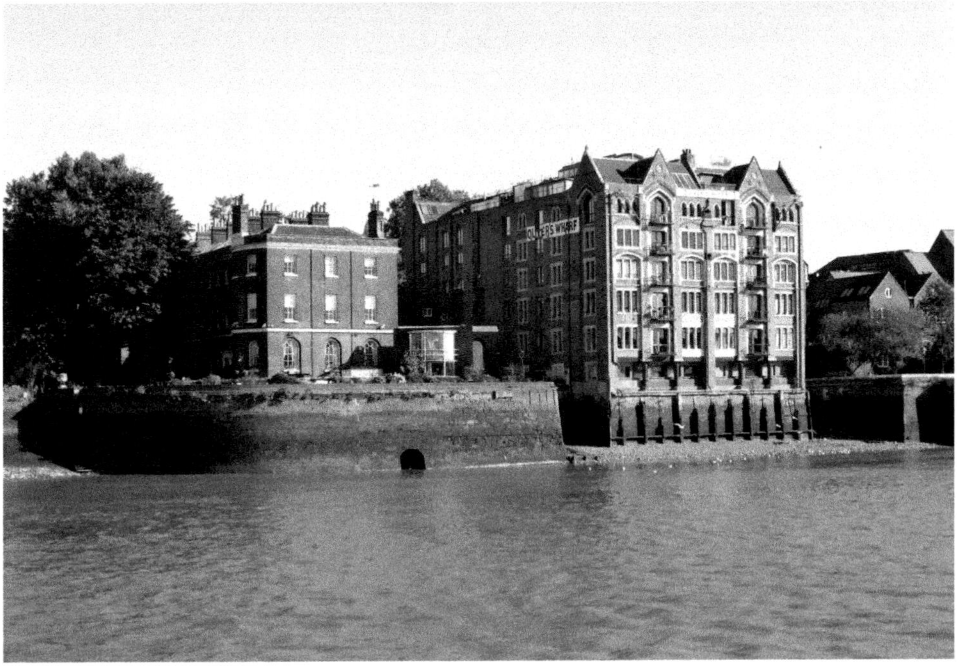

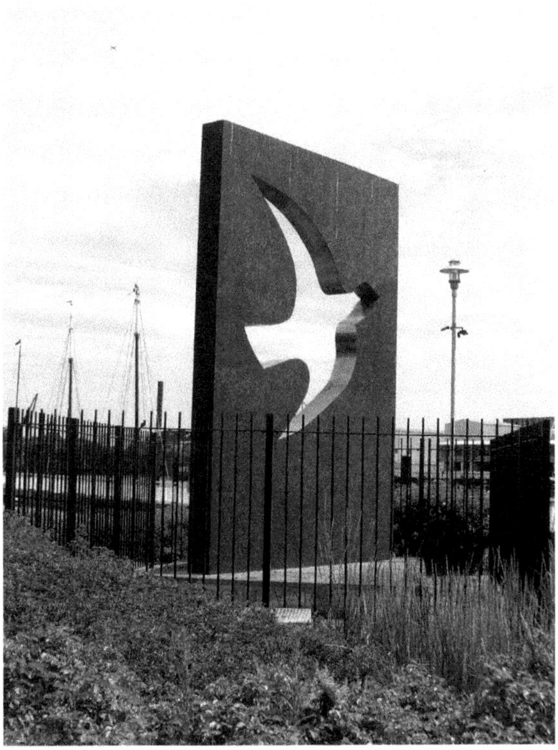

Above: Oliver's Wharf, next to the St Katharine Dock Dockmaster's House, is now converted to housing, and is one of the most attractive on the river. This dates from 1869/70.

Right: By the beginning of Wapping High Street is the Hermitage Riverside Memorial Garden, on the site of Hermitage Wharf, which was hit by a massive firebomb raid on 29 December 1940. Within the garden is a memorial to the East London civilians who were killed and injured during the Second World War. The memorial by Wendy Taylor CBE shows the form of an absent dove to signify the loved ones who were lost.

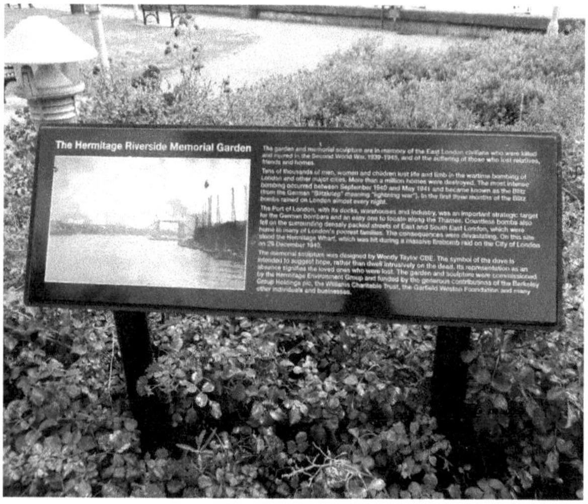

The plaque that accompanies the Hermitage Gardens memorial.

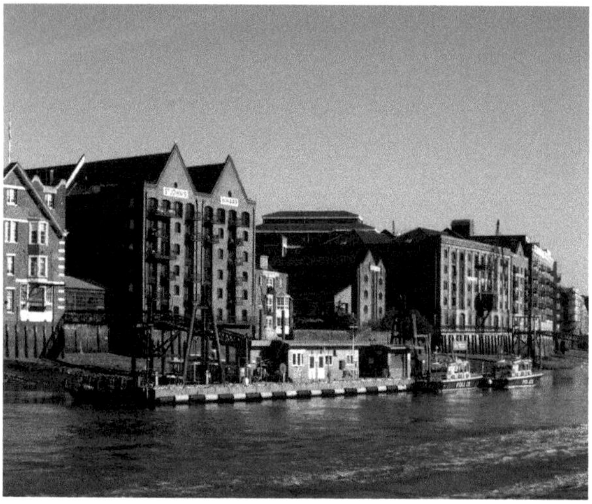

In front of the former St John's Wharf is the Metropolitan Police river police station. There has been a Marine Police Office in this area since 1798. Near to this building there used to be an area known as Execution Dock. There was a gibbet permanently set up, and many pirates and other criminals met their end here. One of the most notorious of these was Captain William Kidd, who was found guilty of piracy in 1701.

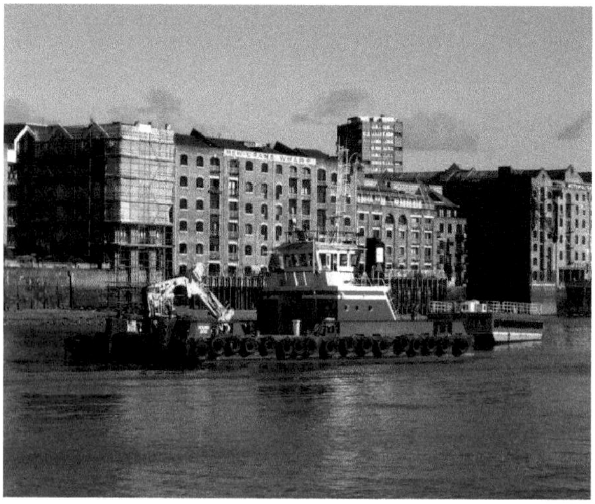

The riverbank at Wapping is lined with former wharves now converted to luxury flats. Seen here from the river are New Crane Wharf and, beyond that, Metropolitan Wharf. A work boat, the *Hound Dog*, is moored on the river, having been involved in maintenance work.

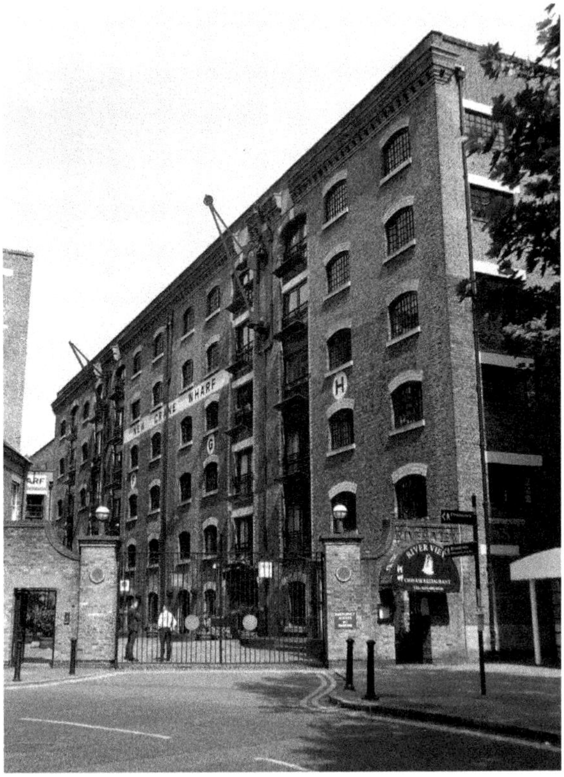

Right: The landward side of New Crane Wharf, which is now a gated complex of apartments. Note how some of the wall-mounted cranes have been retained to add to the appeal.

Below: Along Wapping High Street is Wapping Pier Head, a row of Georgian houses built for dock officials in the early nineteenth century. One of these is the old Customs House, located by the entrance to the London Docks.

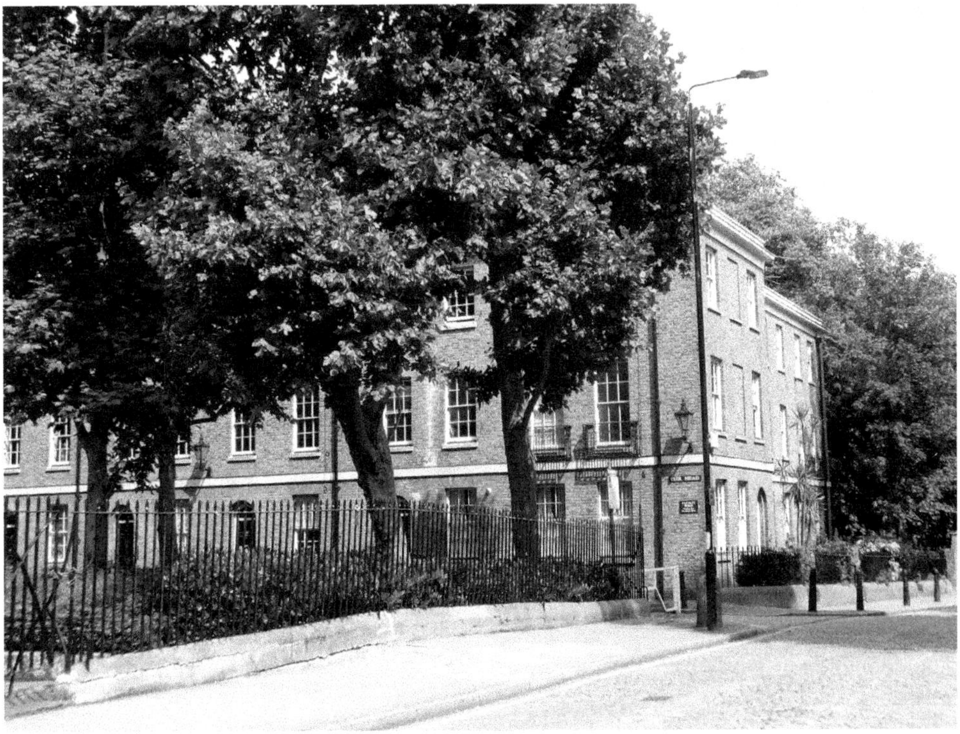

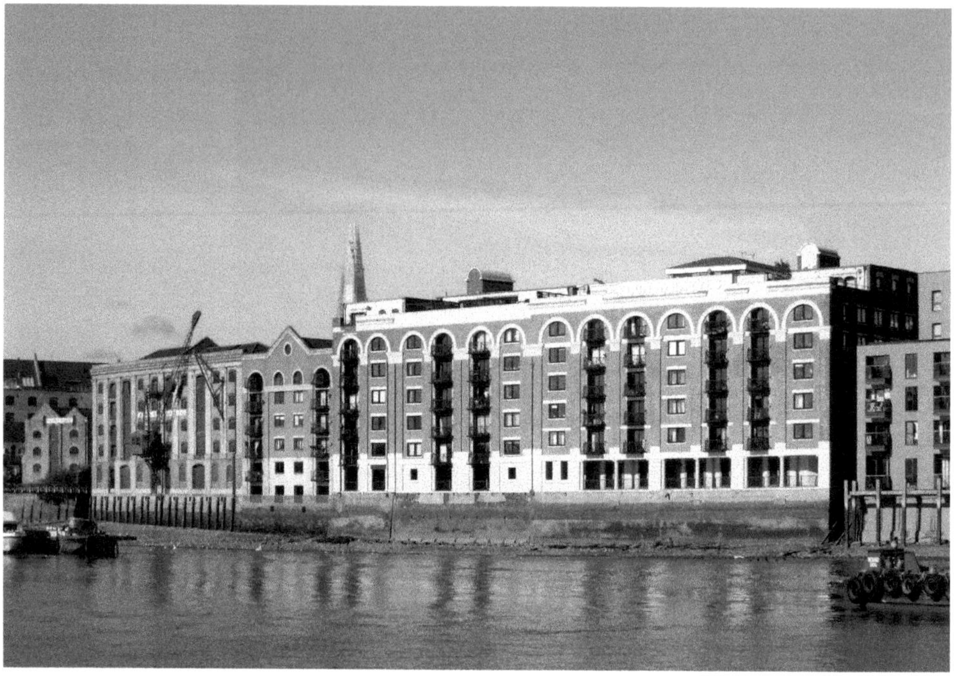

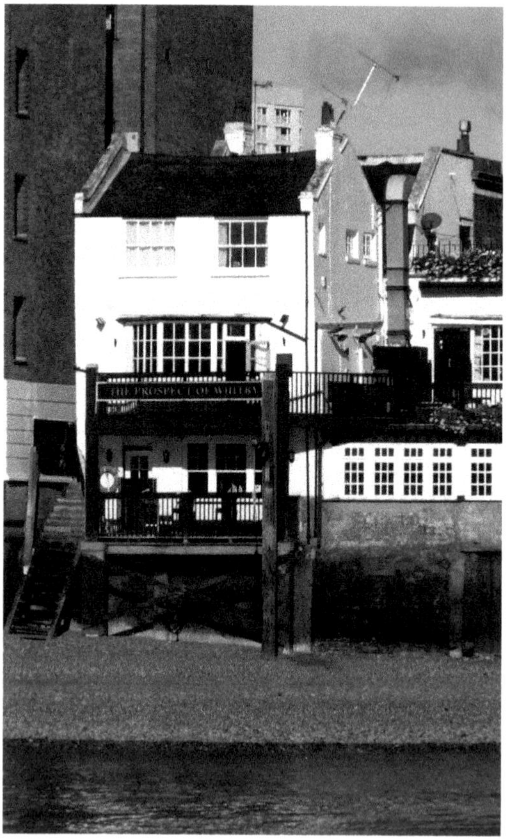

Above: A view of Gun Wharves and King Henry's Wharf, Wapping. Both are now converted to housing, but King Henry's Wharf retains its wall-mounted cranes.

Left: Most famous of the riverside public houses is the Prospect of Whitby. There has been a pub here since around 1520 when it was known as the Devil's Tavern, but the present building dates from the early nineteenth century. The name derives from that of an early collier. Note the stairs giving access to/from the foreshore.

London Docks/Shadwell Basin

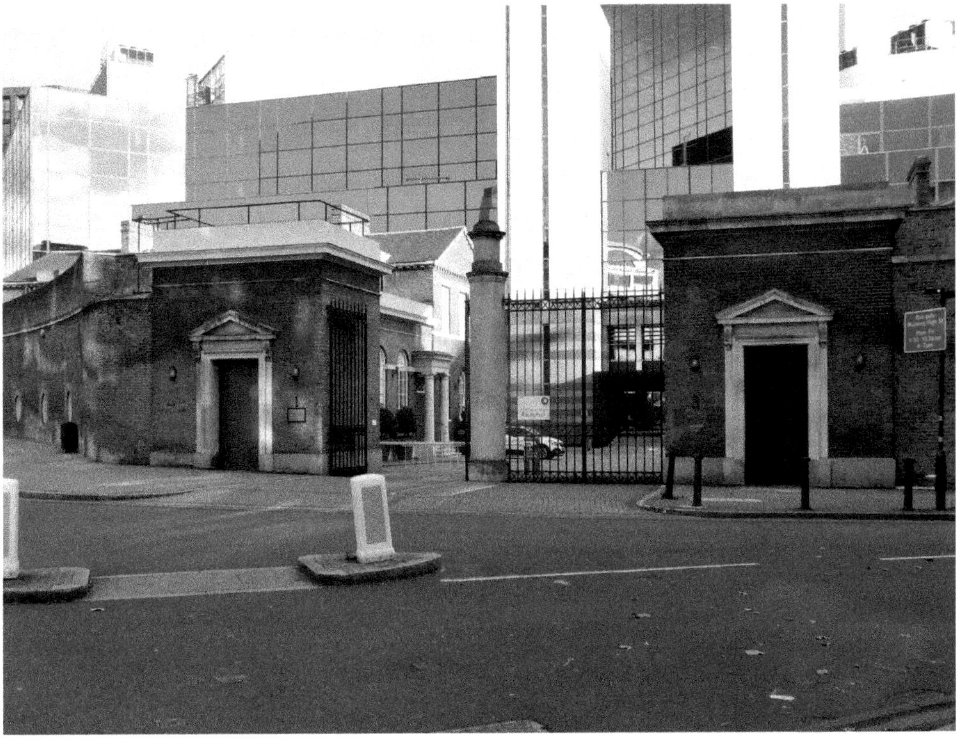

Above: These gates on The Highway formerly gave access to London Docks but now lead to modern office buildings.

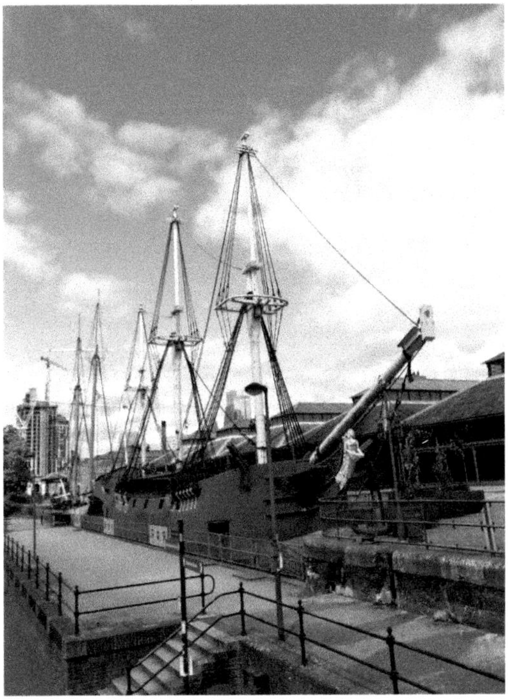

Right: Tobacco Dock, part of London Docks. After closure, there was an attempt to develop Tobacco Dock as a tourist market to rival Covent Garden. This opened in 1989 but was not successful. The site fell derelict and during 2012 was used to house soldiers brought in to protect London during the Olympic Games. The Grade I listed warehouse, built 1811–14, is now used as an events venue space. The illustration shows the *Three Sisters*, one of two 'pirate ships' permanently displayed here since the time of the tourist market. They were reminders of some of the ships that used to unload cargo here.

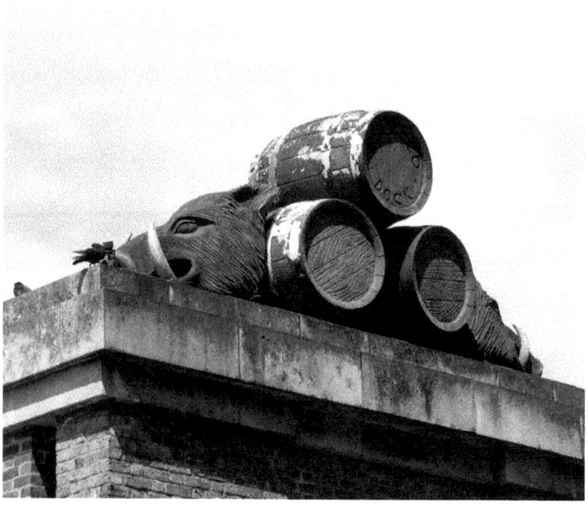

Over the entrance to Tobacco Dock in Wapping Lane, the boar's heads and barrels are a reminder of some of the goods passing through this dock. Wines, spice, ivory and animal furs were common commodities unloaded here alongside tobacco.

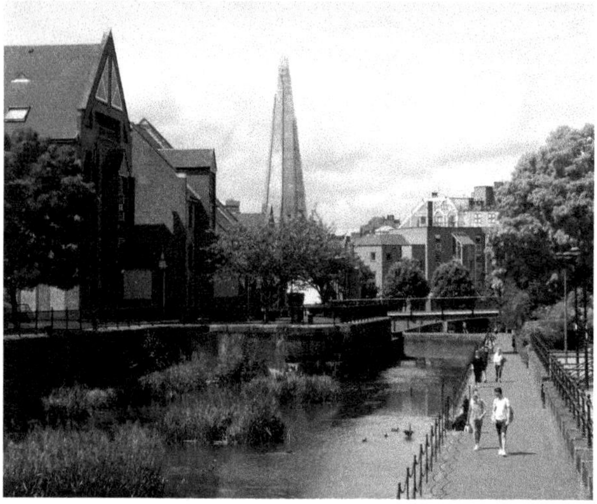

The Ornamental Canal is a non-navigable waterway created between the St Katharine Dock and Shadwell Basin areas, where much of the original London Docks have been filled in. This view from near Shadwell Basin and looking west has the Shard prominent in the distance.

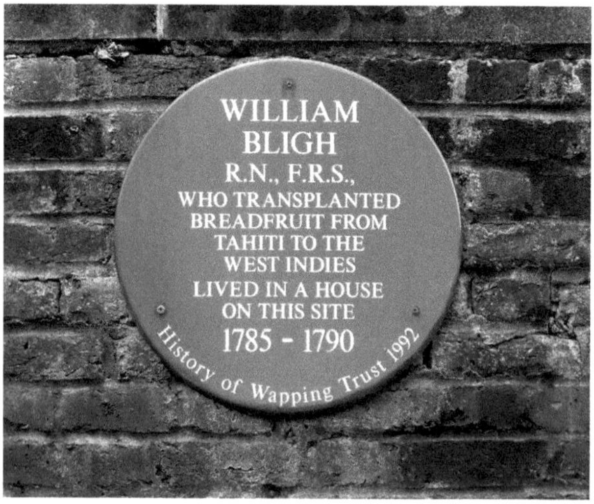

In Rearden Street off Wapping Lane, this blue plaque is mounted on a brick wall. The house itself no longer survives. Captain Bligh commanded a ship on one of Captain Cook's voyages. But he is best known as the commander of HMS *Bounty* when some of the crew mutinied. He was set adrift in a small open boat with eighteen of the crew and successfully navigated it without maps across the Pacific Ocean to Timor, a journey of some 3,600 miles that lasted forty-five days.

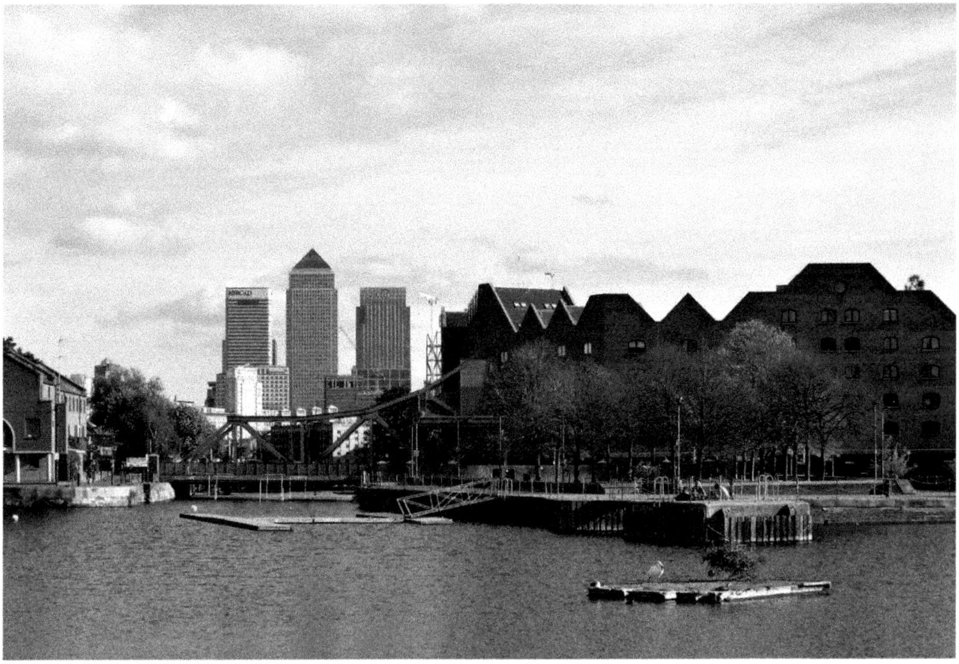

Shadwell Basin looking east. This is the only part of the former London Docks to retain its waters. In the distance are the towers of the Canary Wharf financial district.

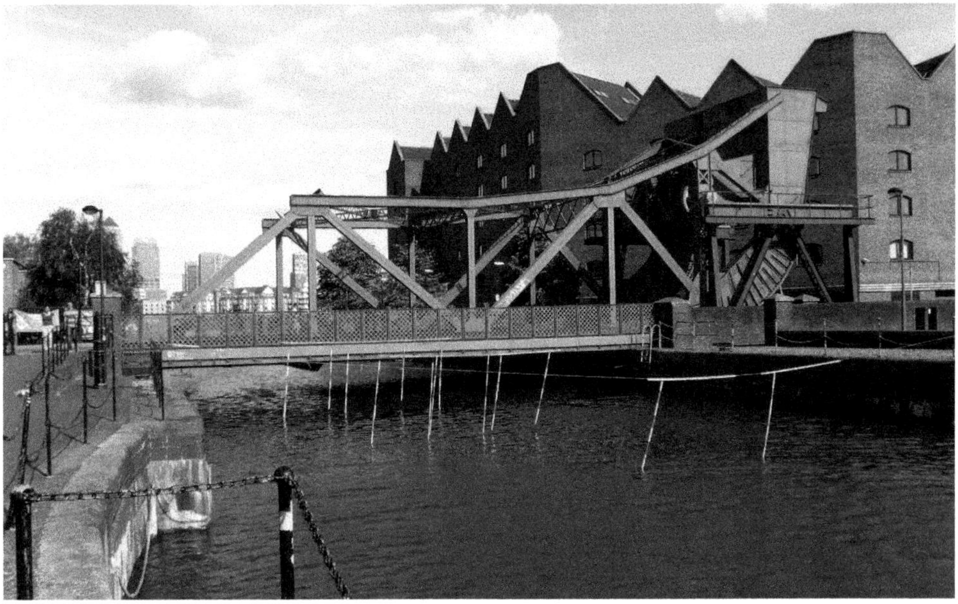

This now disused lifting bridge allowed traffic on Glamis Road to cross the access to Shadwell Basin. This view is from 2013. This bridge used to swing upwards to let ships enter. The hydraulic power to raise the bridge was provided by the nearby London Hydraulic Power Company. The large metal structure at the near end of the bridge in the photo is a tank that was filled with water to provide the counter-balance weight for the roadway.

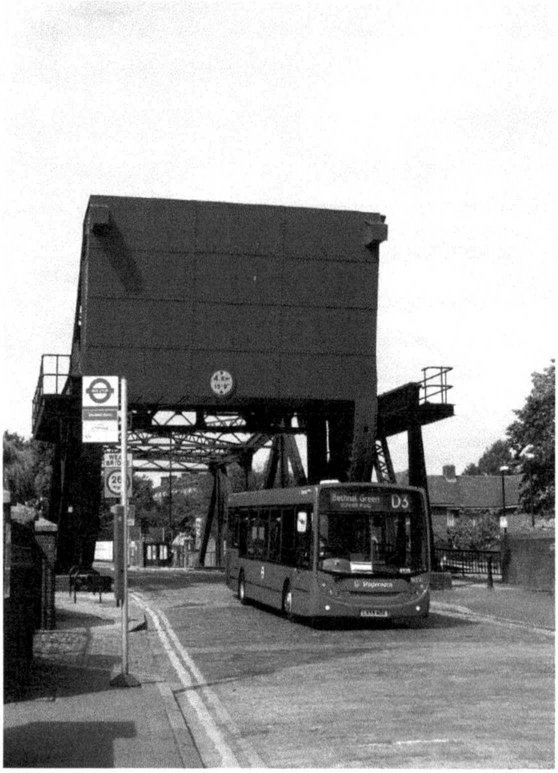

Left: Moving on to 2020 and the bridge has had a repaint. Bus route D3 is routed over the bridge and then along Wapping Wall.

Below: The 1890 Wapping pumping station of the London Hydraulic Power Company in Wapping Wall. This remained in use until 1977, being the last in operational use, and is Grade II listed. This was sold by the LDDC to a trust led by Australian impresario Jules Wright for £75,000 in 1992. Despite being turned down for lottery funding, it reopened in October 2000 as the Wapping Project – an arts centre and restaurant complex. Some of the original equipment remains inside.

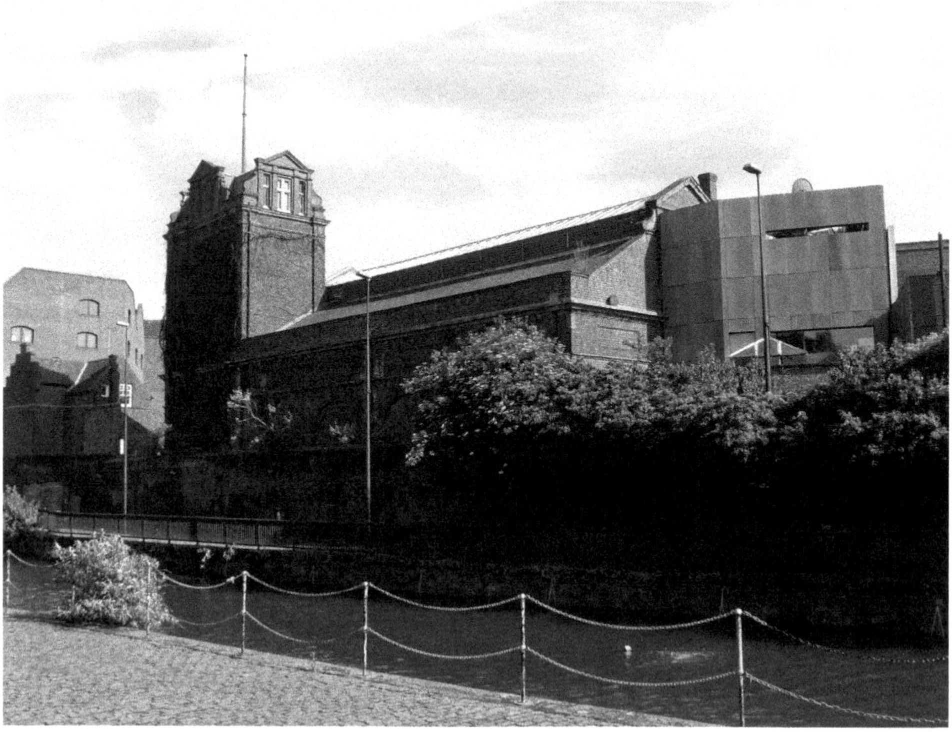

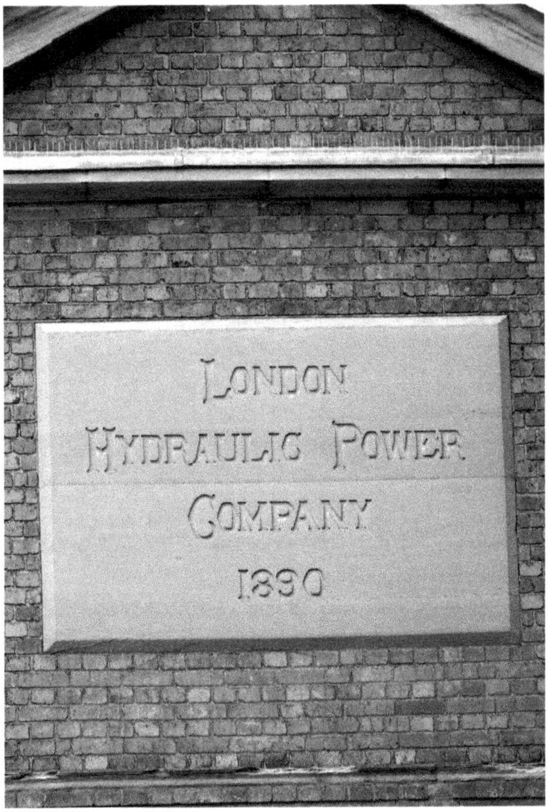

Right: The plaque on the pumping station accumulator tower. Hydraulic power was first introduced into the docks in 1852 by William Armstrong of Newcastle. The pumps used to fill the tower were driven by steam engines. As the water filled the tower it raised a weighted plunger usually filled with gravel, which built up pressure at the base to about 700 pounds per square inch. It was called an accumulator because water was pumped in during off-peak times and was stored to provide power in busy periods. The water was piped to provide hydraulic power to work the cranes, capstans, bridges and lock gates in the docks.

Below: The entrance lock to Shadwell Basin is home to the Shadwell Basin Outdoor Activity Centre, offering a range of water-based activities.

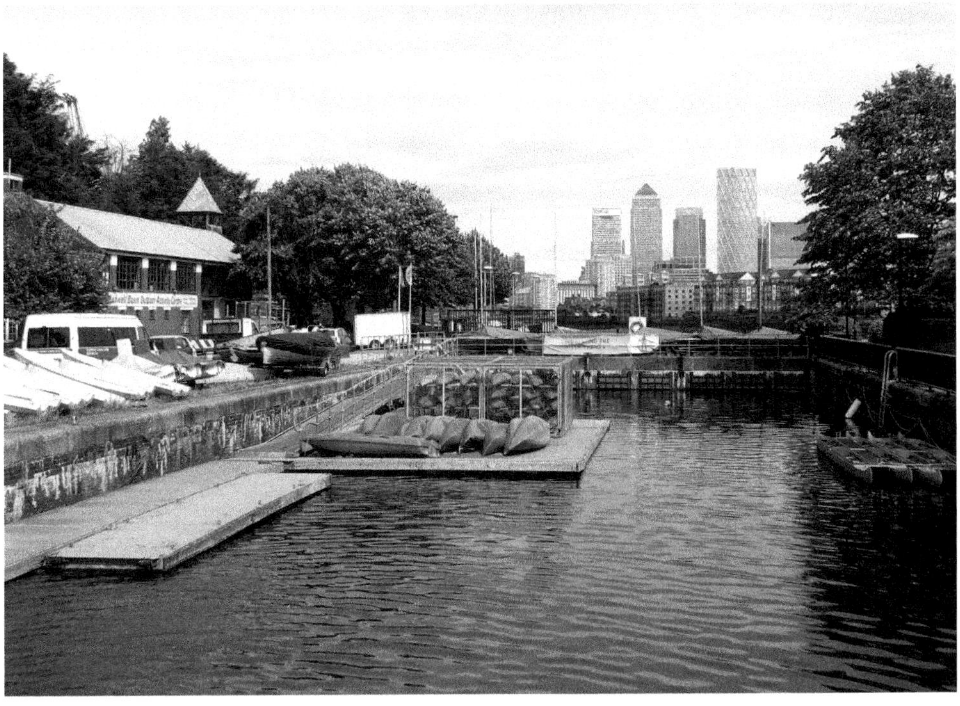

Stepney and to Limehouse Basin/Regent's Canal Docks

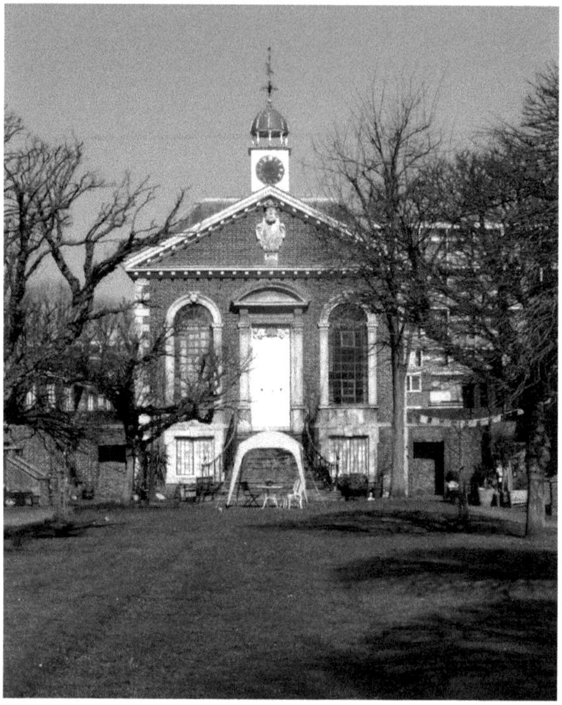

Left: Trinity Almshouses on Mile End Road, Stepney, date back to 1695 and are particularly relevant here as they were intended for mariners and their widows who had fallen on hard times. The architect was William Ogbourne.

Below: A plaque on the almshouses. This reads: 'This Almes House wherein 28 decay'd Masters and Comanders of Ships or y Widows of such are maintain'd was built by y CORP. of Trinity House An. 1695. The ground was given by Capt. HENRY MUDD of Rattcliff an Elder Brother whose Widow did also contribute'.

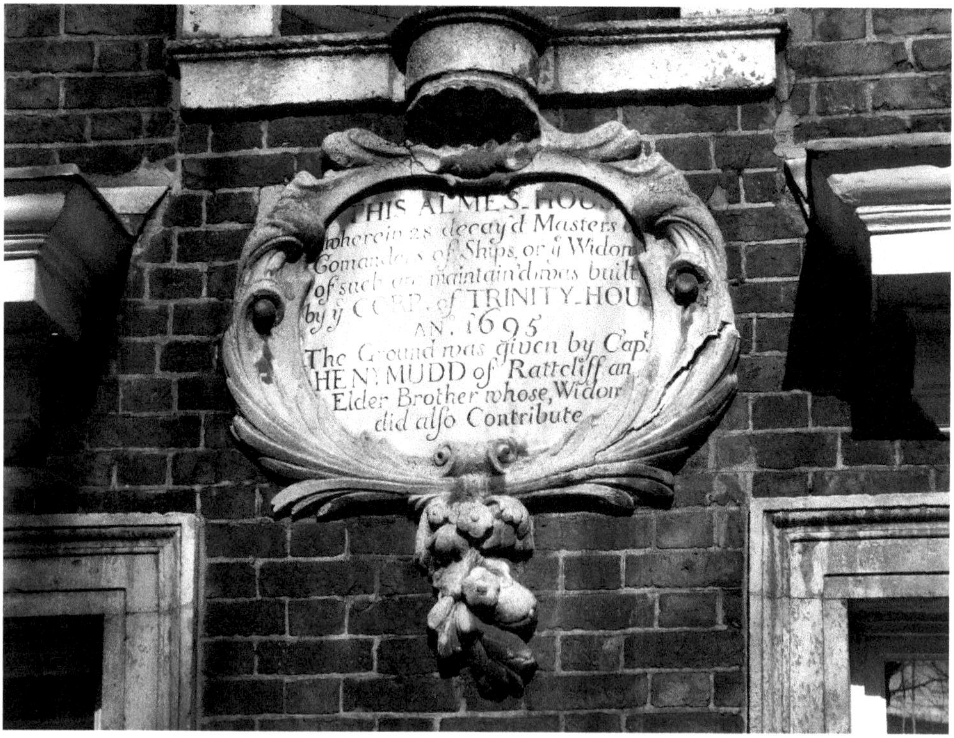

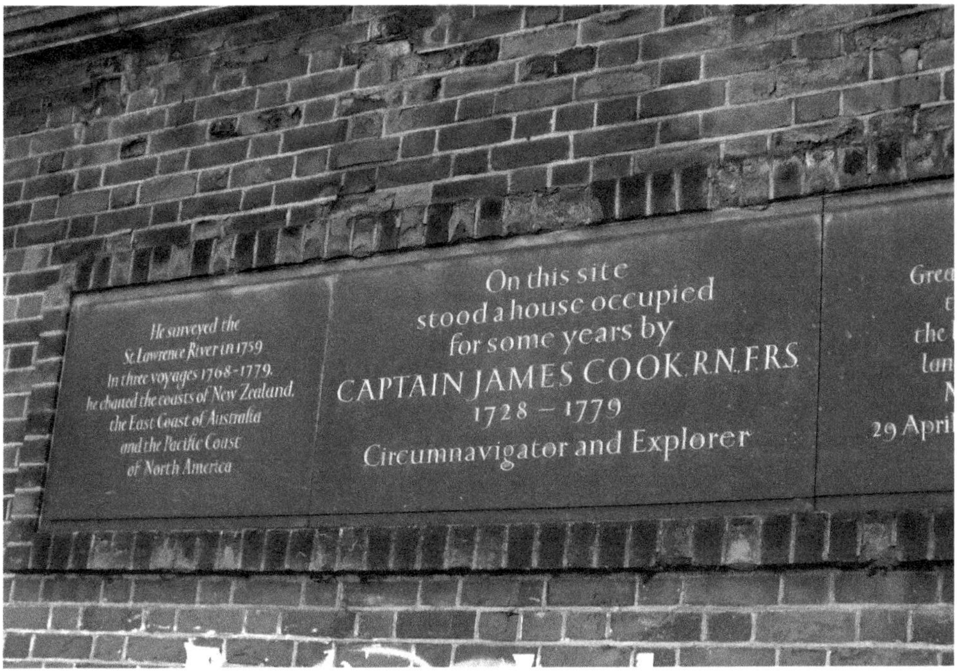

Nearby, at No. 88 Mile End Road, an inscription on a wall informs us that a house once occupied by Captain James Cook RN, FRS formerly stood on the site. In his day this would have been a semi-rural location, but within easy reach of the Thames and the City of London.

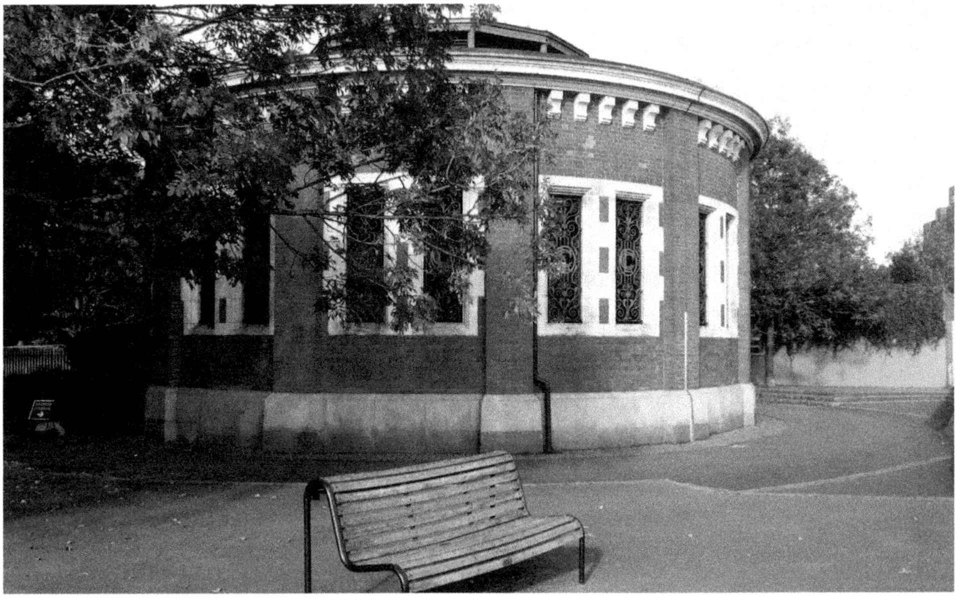

In King Edward Memorial Park, Shadwell, the northern ventilation and access shaft to the Rotherhithe tunnel can be found. The building bears the monogram of the London County Council. A similar shaft can be found on the south bank (see p. 69). Thames Water are constructing a ventilation tower nearby for their Thames Tideway tunnel.

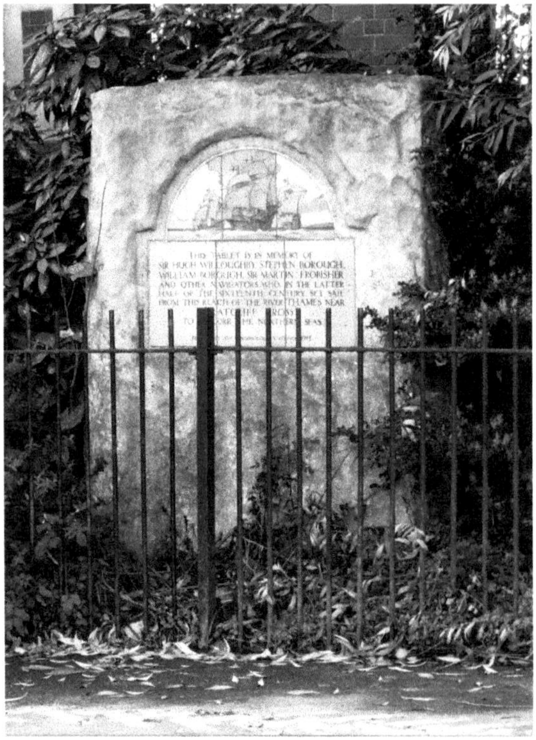

The Willoughby memorial tablet is situated just behind the tunnel ventilation shaft and is in ceramic tiles. The tablet reads: 'This tablet is in memory of Sir Hugh Willoughby, Stephen Borough, William Borough, Sir Martin Frobisher and other navigators who in the latter half of the sixteenth century set sail from this reach of the River Thames near Ratcliff Cross to explore the northern seas.' It was erected by the London County Council in 1922.

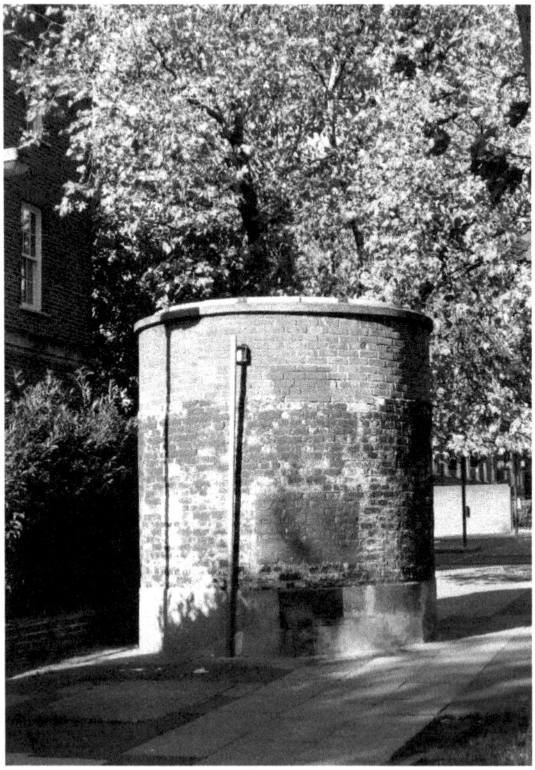

This curious construction is a ventilation shaft for Brunel's Thames tunnel of 1825–43, now part of the London Overground railway network (see p. 66).

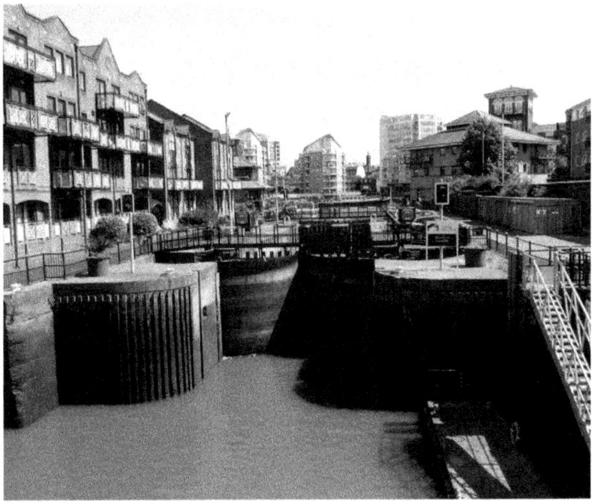

The entry lock to Limehouse Basin, which gives access from the Thames to the canal system. The photograph is taken from the road swing bridge on Narrow Street.

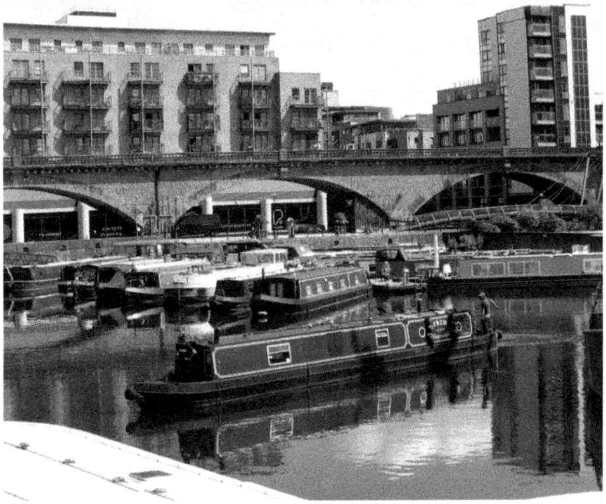

Limehouse Basin has been developed as a marina surrounded by modern housing. There are usually a large number of canal narrowboats moored here and sometimes also Thames barges. The viaduct was originally built for the London & Blackwall Railway and is now used by the Docklands Light Railway.

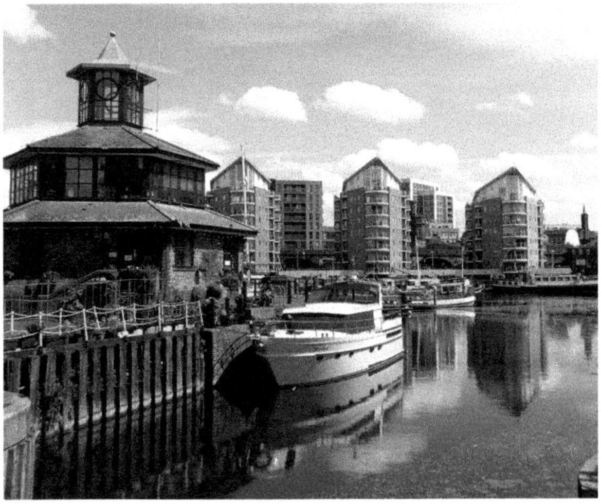

Another view of Limehouse Basin looking west.

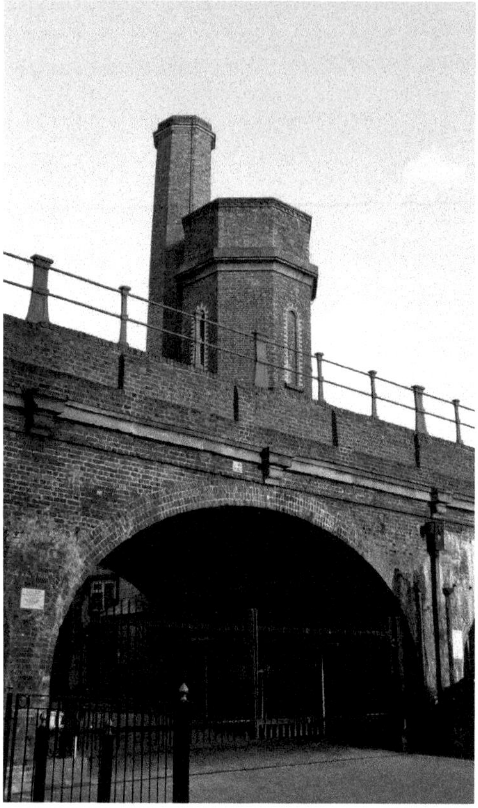

Left: Alongside the Docklands Light Railway is this accumulator tower in Mill Place, off Commercial Road. This octagonal tower, built in 1869, was used to store water that provided the hydraulic power for the cranes and locks in the nearby Limehouse Basin. The water was stored in a cylinder capped by heavy weight. Water was pumped into the cylinder raising the 80-ton weight containing gravel, which put the water under a pressure of about 700 pounds per square inch.

Below: This large building on Limehouse Road and Salmon Lane is the Sailors' Society Seamen's Mission. This was built in 1923/4 as the Empire Memorial Sailor's Hostel and opened by Princess Marie Louise, one of Queen Victoria's granddaughters. The architects were Thomas Brammall Daniel and Horace Parnacott. It was extended in Salmon Lane in 1932. The Sailors' Society has its origins in the Port of London Society, founded in 1818, and is now a global Christian charity working in ports across the world. The mission has now been converted into private apartments since 1994.

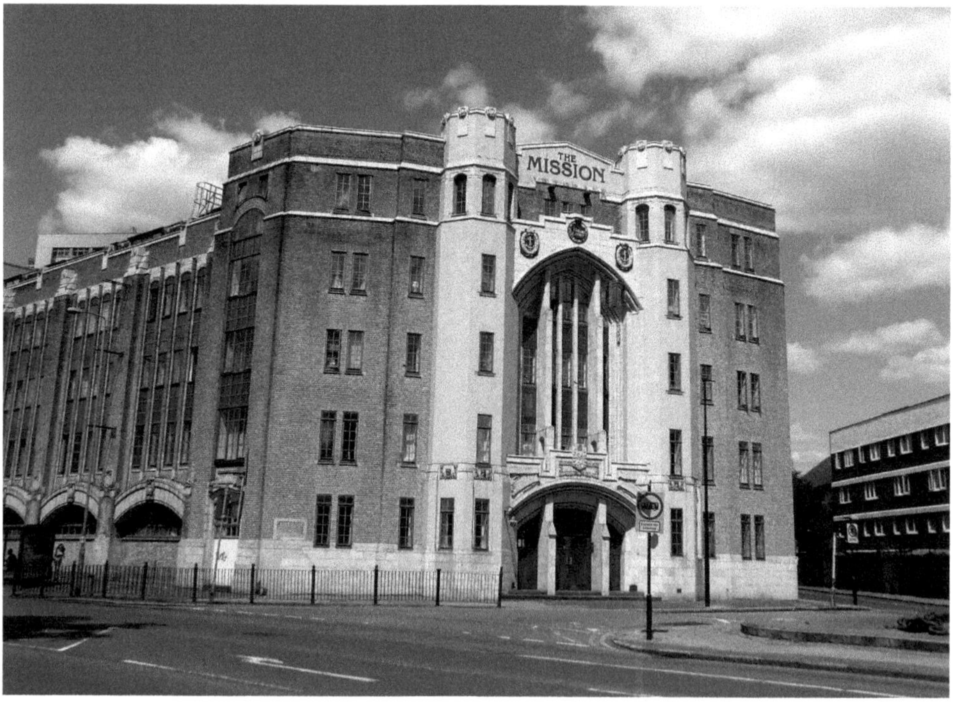

Regent's Canal Docks and its Offshoots

Regent's Canal celebrated its 200th anniversary in 2020, having been opened on 1 August 1820. It was named after the Prince Regent, later King George IV, during whose rule the canal was started in 1812. Joining the Thames at Limehouse Basin, it threads through east London round to Islington, then running west to Paddington Basin where it connects to the Grand Union Canal. It enabled goods such as coal and building materials brought in by sea to be transported onwards by barge and lighters around London and up to the Midlands. Nowadays the canals are used for leisure boating and increasingly by houseboats, while the towpaths are frequented by walkers, joggers and cyclists.

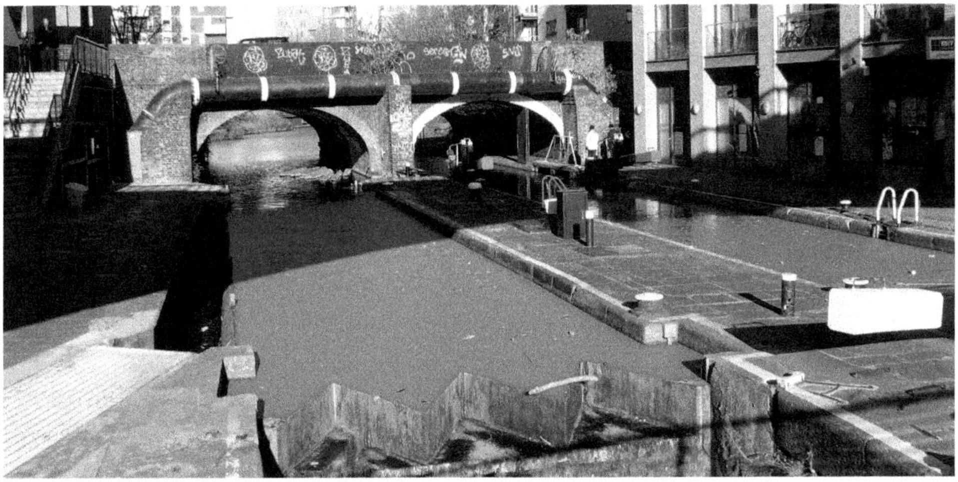

This is Commercial Road Lock, the entrance lock from Limehouse Basin to Regent's Canal.

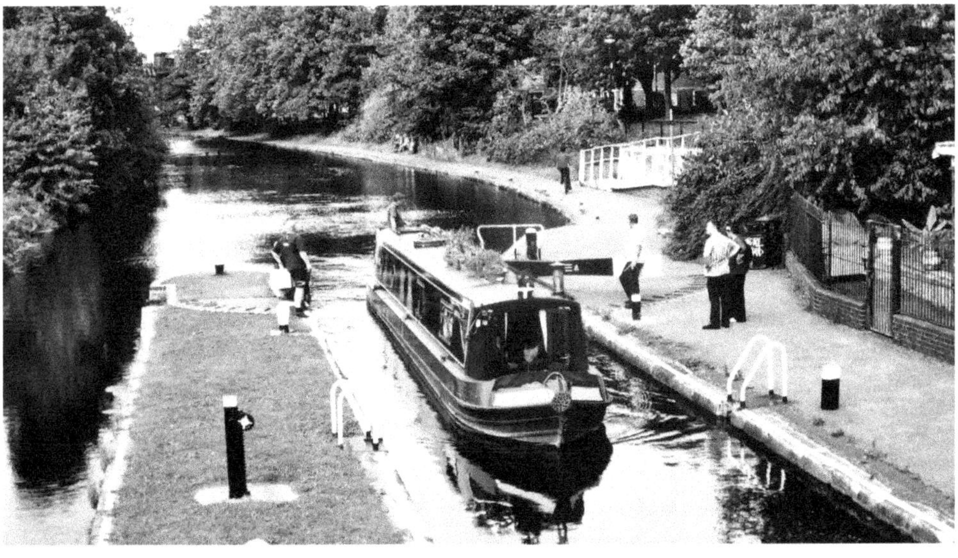

The next to be navigated is the Salmon Lane Lock, here being entered by a narrowboat.

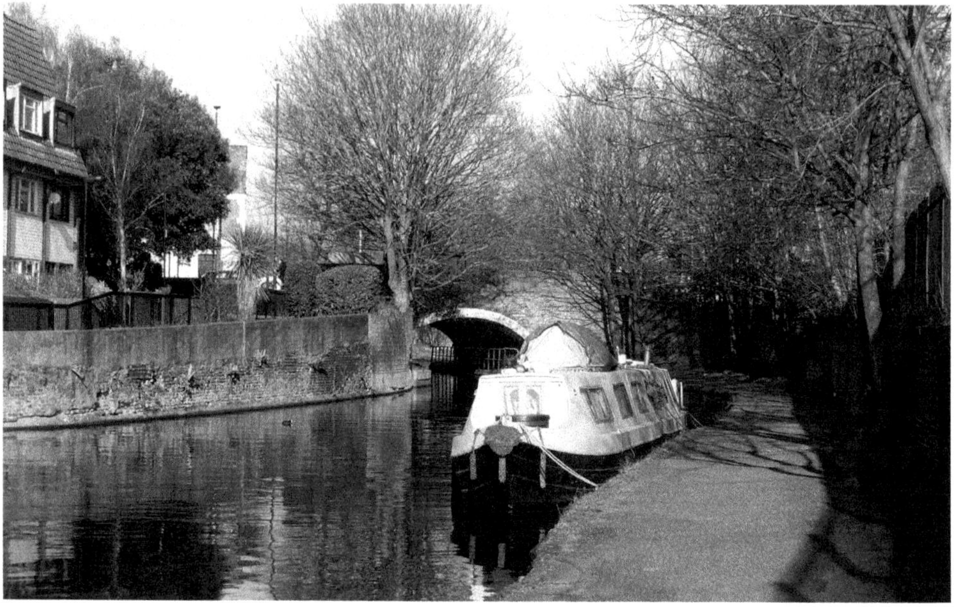

The Regent's Canal continues northwards. After Johnson's Lock, Mile End Park is on the right. This was created in the 1990s from wasteland that had resulted from wartime bombing raids. The scenery approaching Mile End appears quite tranquil, but the bridge under which the canal passes carries the main A11 Mile End Road eastwards from London.

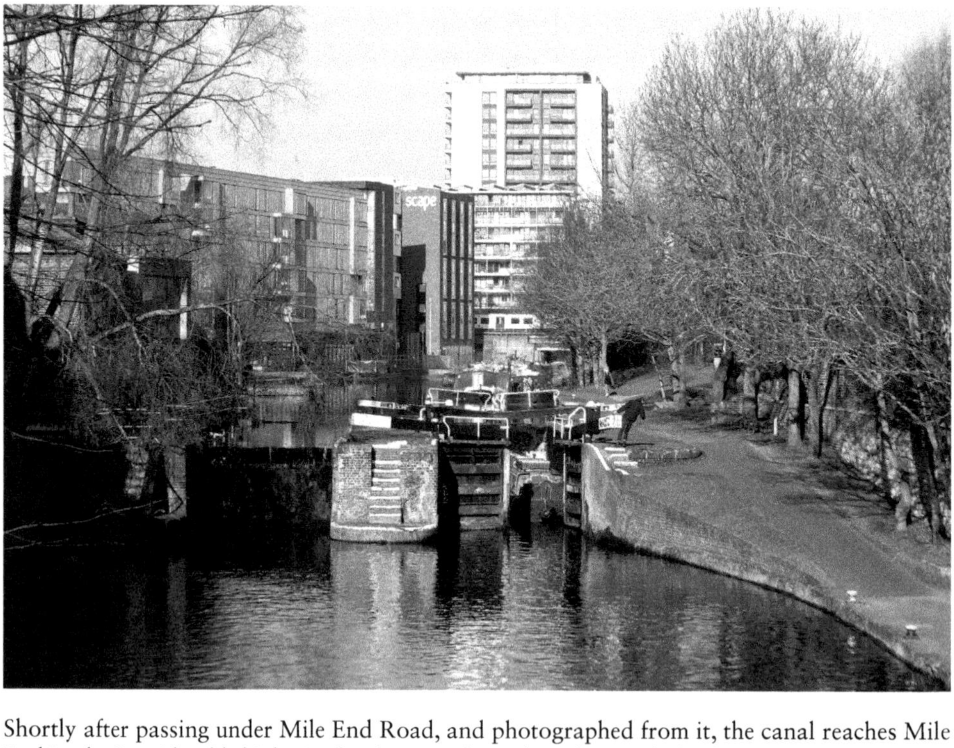

Shortly after passing under Mile End Road, and photographed from it, the canal reaches Mile End Lock. Considerable high-rise development has taken place in the background in recent years.

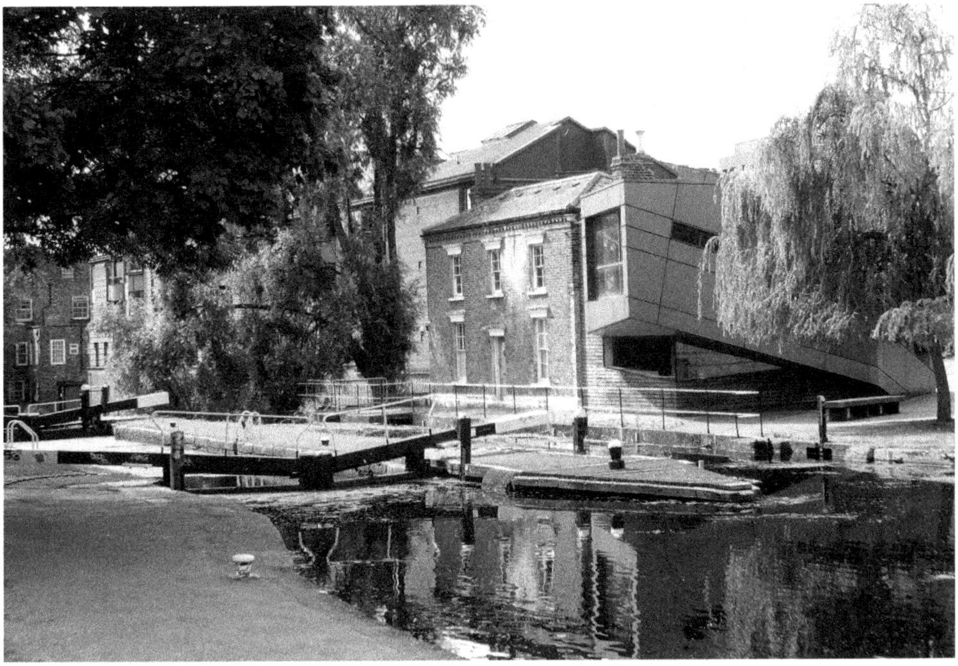

The lock-keeper's house provided at Mile End Lock, which now sports a curious modern extension of a very different architectural style.

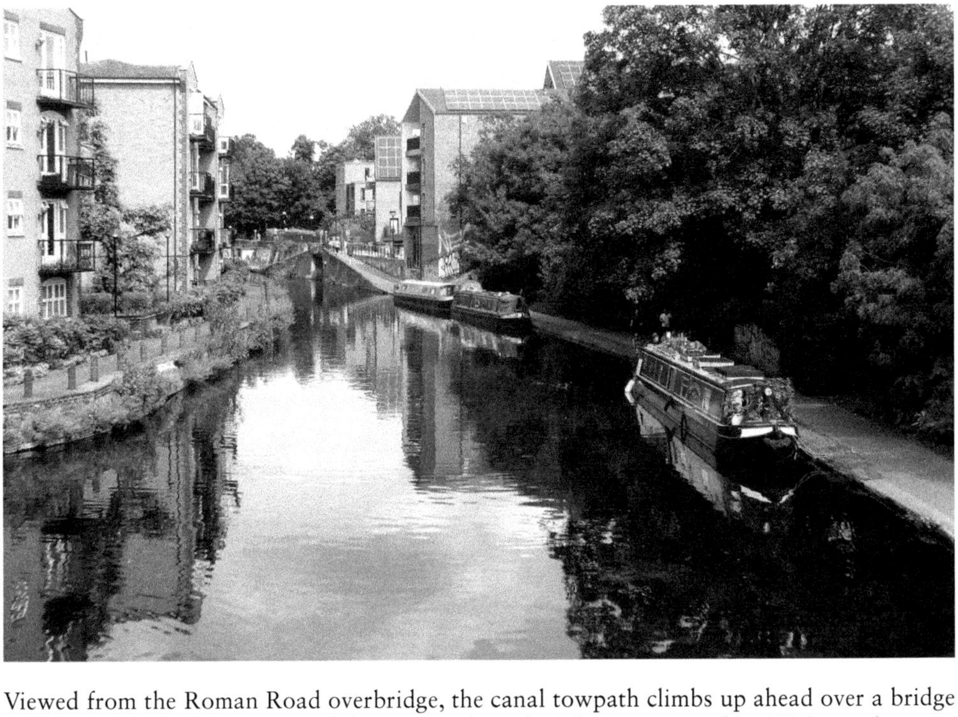

Viewed from the Roman Road overbridge, the canal towpath climbs up ahead over a bridge where the Hertford Union Canal diverges to the right. This was opened in 1830 as a short cut from the Regent's Canal to the River Lea.

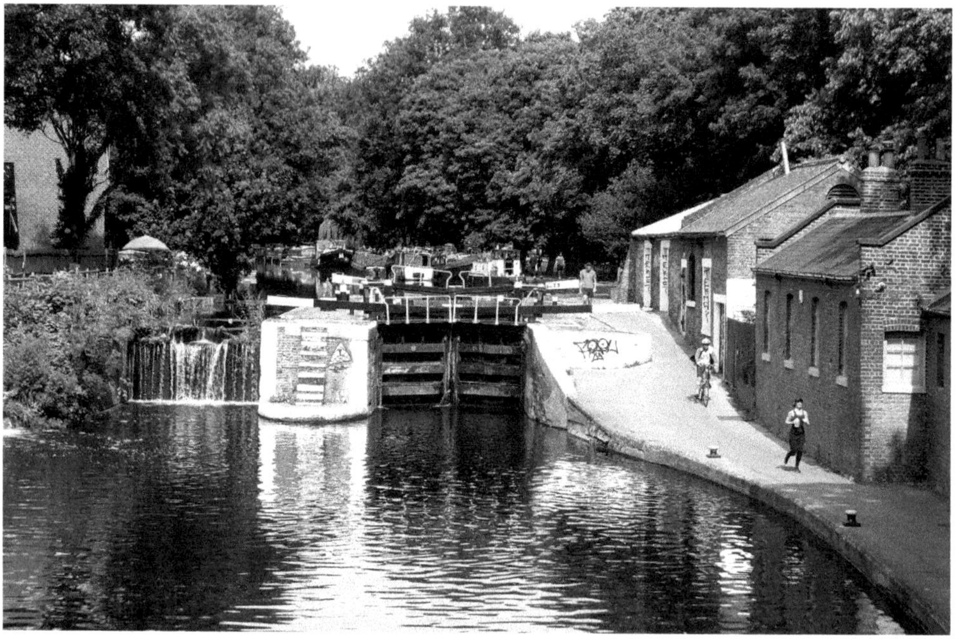

Continuing on the Regent's Canal we come to Old Ford Lock. The towpath is heavily used by joggers and cyclists, as evidenced here. Graffiti is a problem along the towpaths, as it is elsewhere. Victoria Park is on the right-hand side.

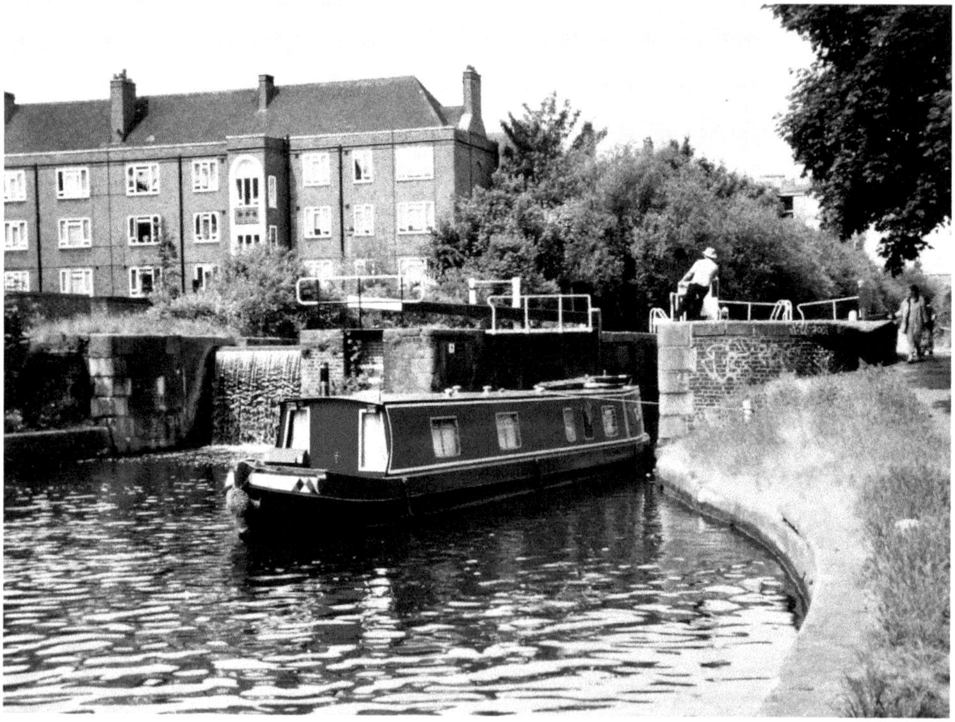

The lock gates are opened for a narrowboat to enter Actons Lock, Hackney.

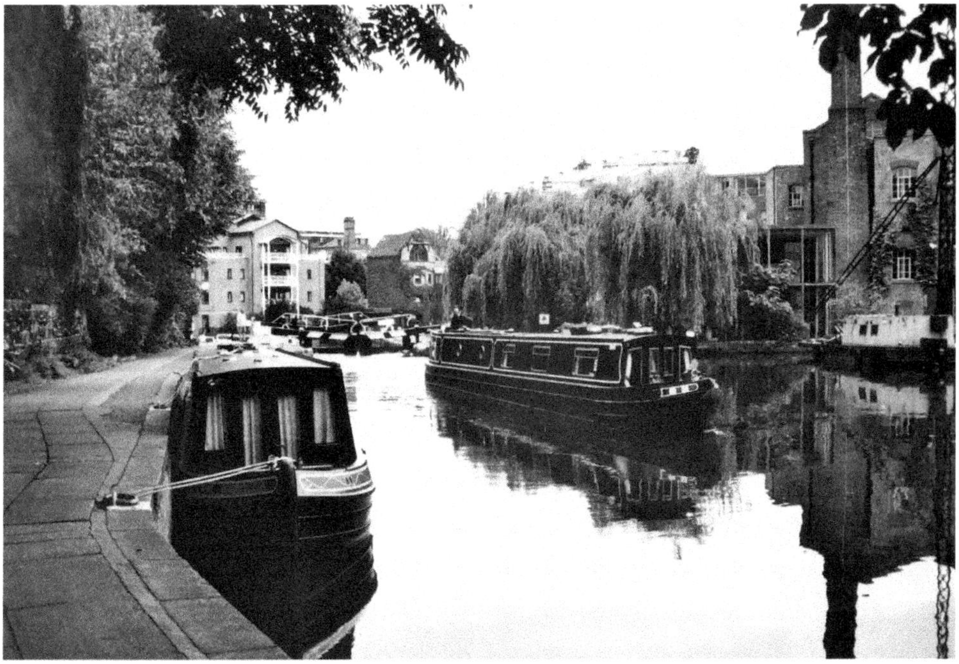

The Regent's Canal turns westward, and then south-westward to reach Islington and the City Road basin and lock.

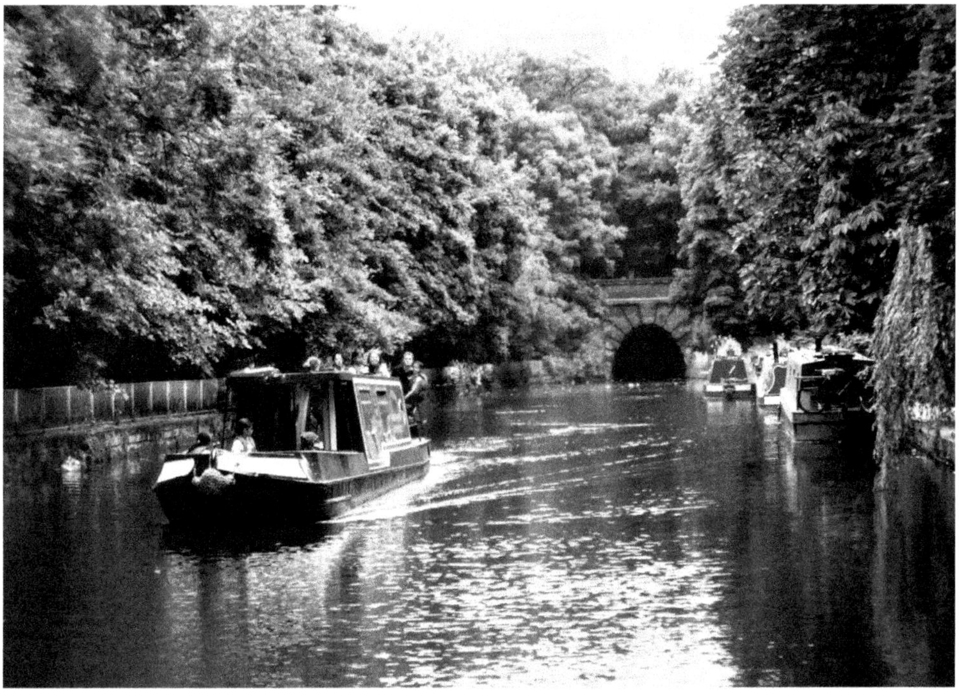

The canal then enters the three-quarter-mile-long Islington tunnel, taking it below the junction of Liverpool Road and Upper Street by Angel station.

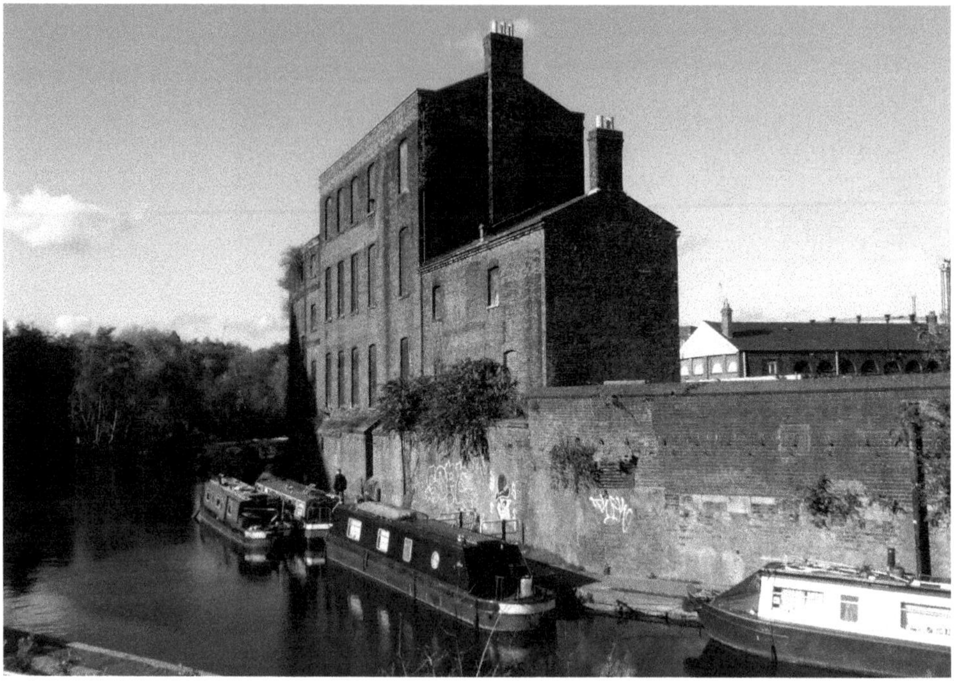

After emerging near Caledonian Road, the canal continues west under York Way. The railway from Kings Cross station tunnels beneath the canal, which now turns north-west towards Camden. It runs past an area around Granary Square once dominated by disused railway goods sheds but has now been redeveloped into a fashionable shopping and eating district. This view is from 2014 and shows former LNER railway buildings awaiting repurposing.

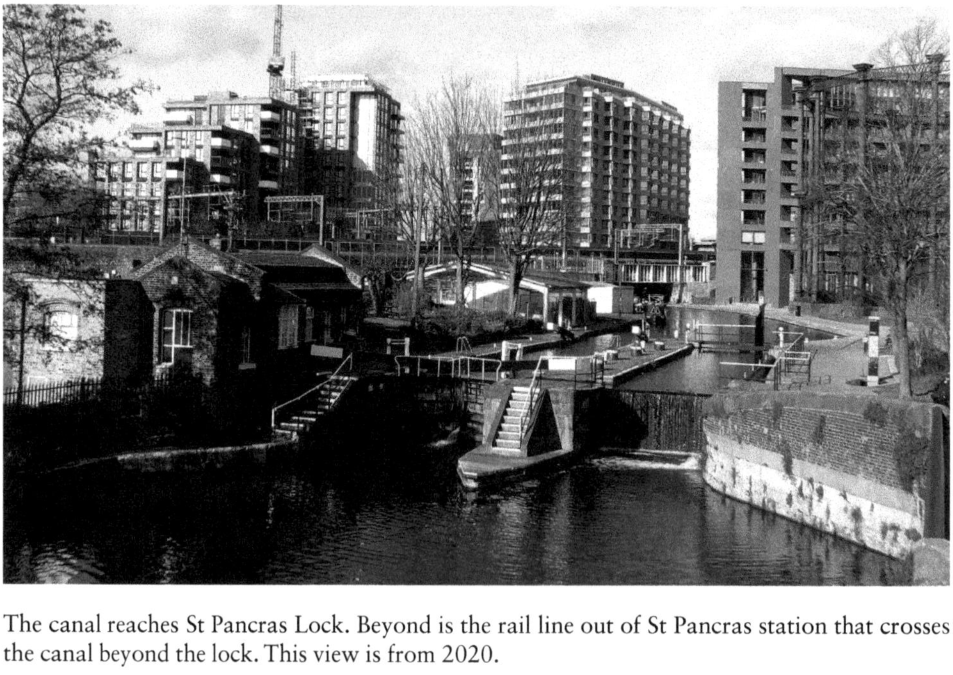

The canal reaches St Pancras Lock. Beyond is the rail line out of St Pancras station that crosses the canal beyond the lock. This view is from 2020.

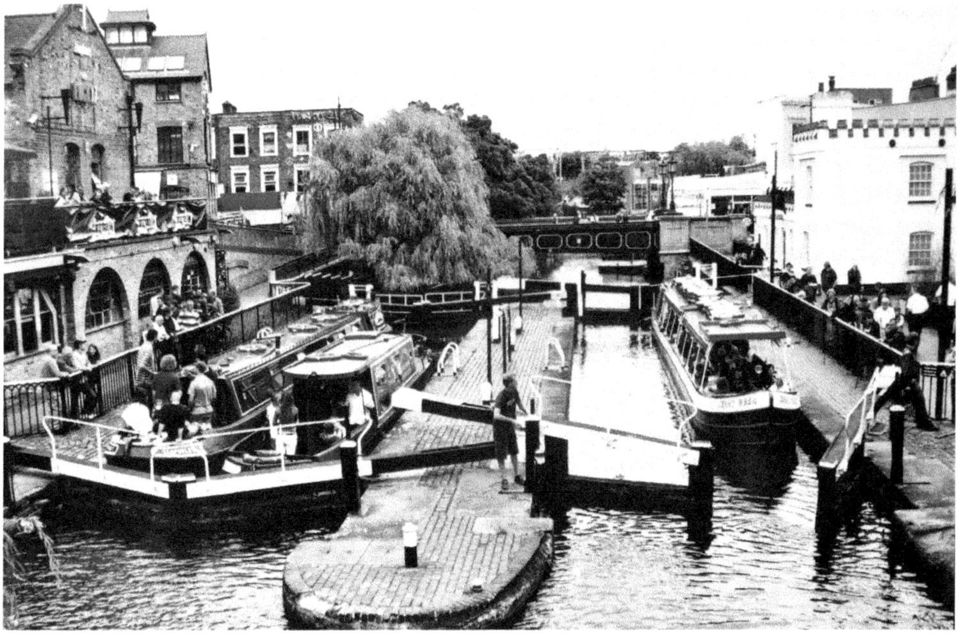

The canal reaches Camden lock, where the adjacent Camden Market is a major tourist attraction. The narrowboat on the right, the *Jenny Wren*, runs tours on this section of the canal onwards past London Zoo towards Paddington Basin, where it will join the Grand Union Canal.

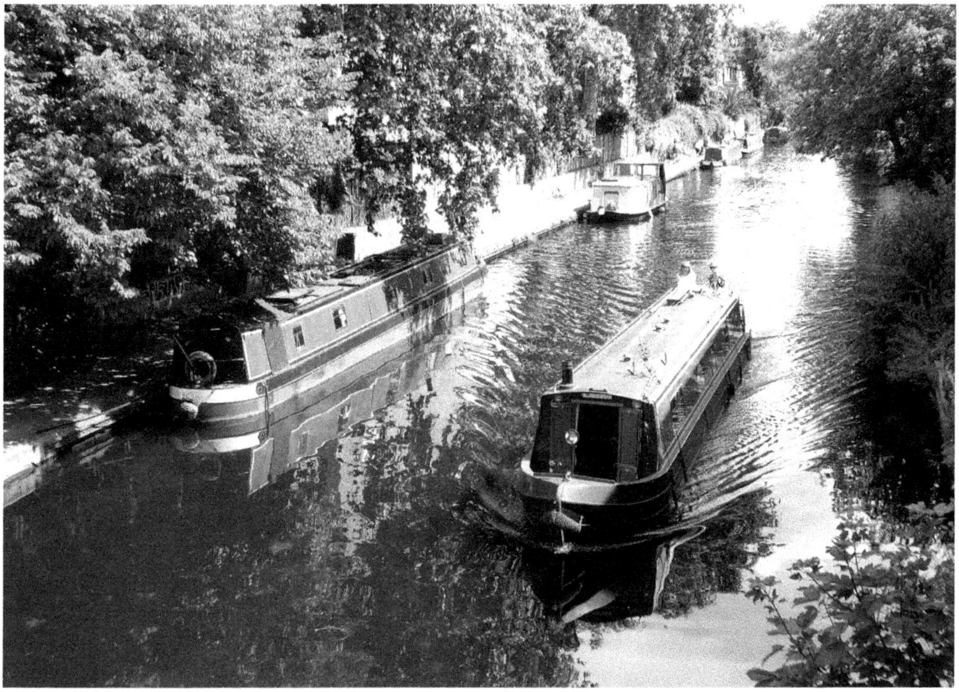

As mentioned earlier, the Hertford Union Canal turns off at Old Ford and runs north-east to join the River Lea. Victoria Park skirts its north bank. A narrowboat is heading west.

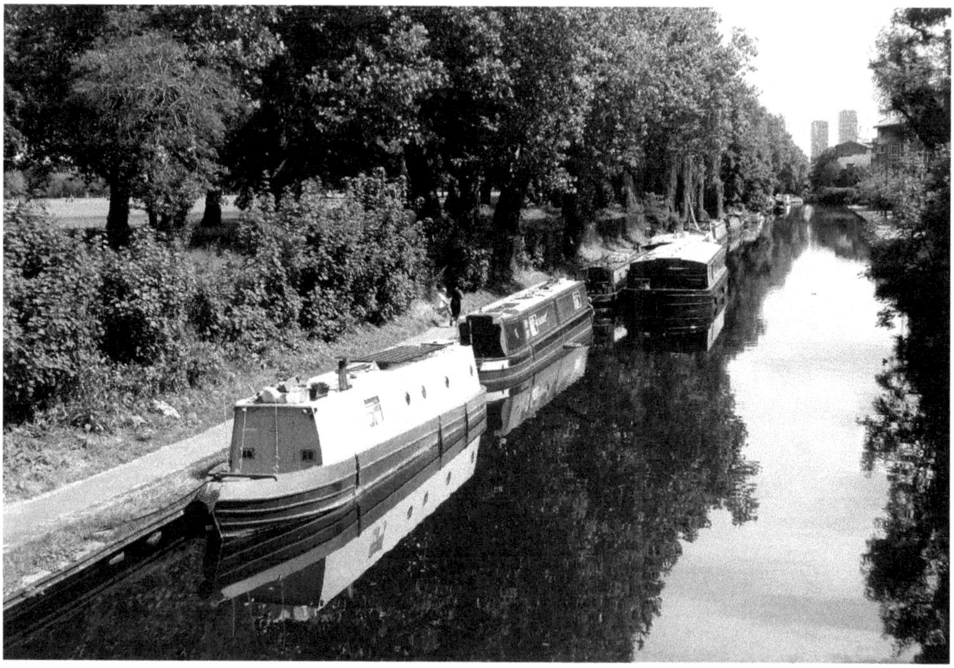

Further along the canal and the park can be seen on the left-hand side. Victoria Park opened in 1845 in response to concerns that the local population had no places for exercise and recreation.

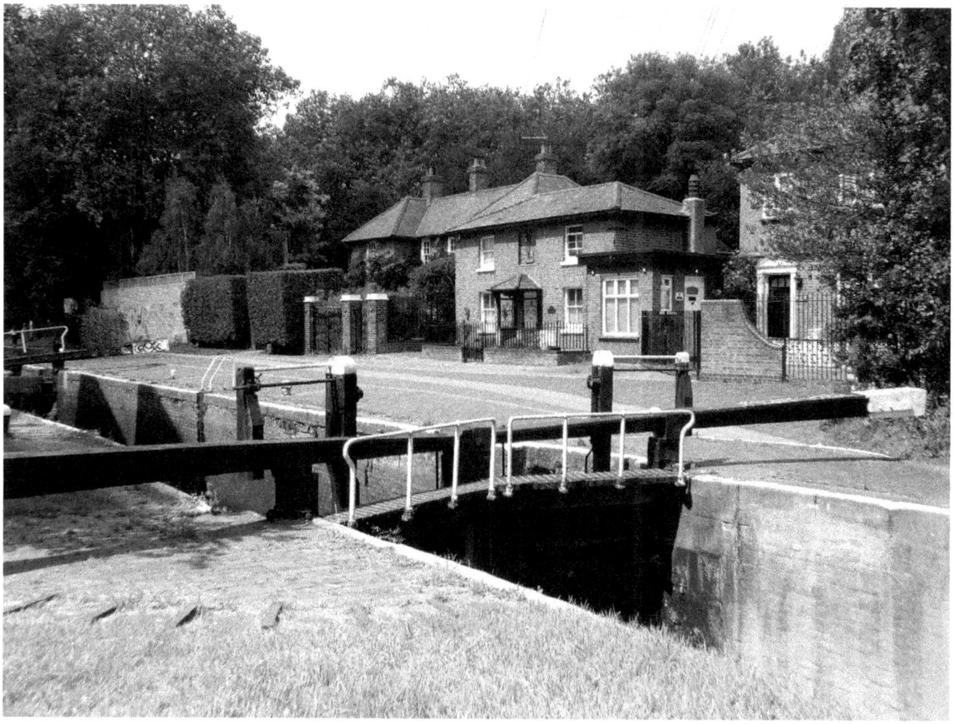

This is the Hertford Union Top Lock with the former lock-keeper's cottage.

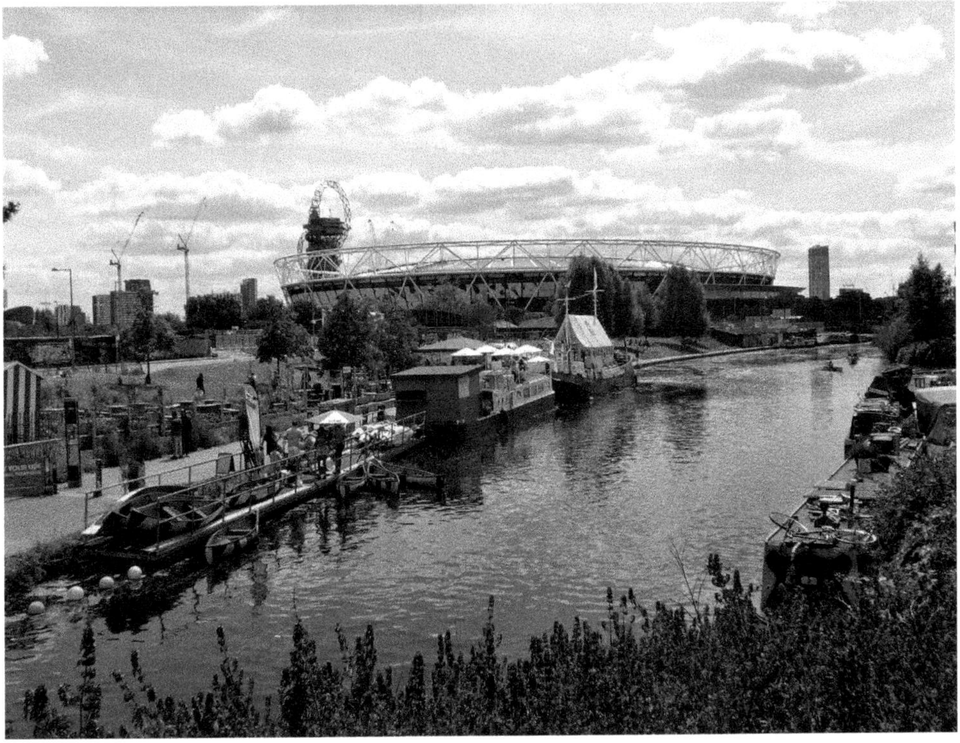

Above: The Hertford Union Canal meets the River Lea Navigation, a cut-off from the river itself created in 1768 to make an easier journey for canal craft, by what is now the Queen Elizabeth Olympic Park, created following the 2012 Olympic Games. The Olympic Stadium, now known as the London Stadium, has become the home of West Ham United FC. Behind that is the Arcellor Mittell Orbit designed by Anish Kapoor. The cranes are evidence of further building developments in this area, now given the postcode E20.

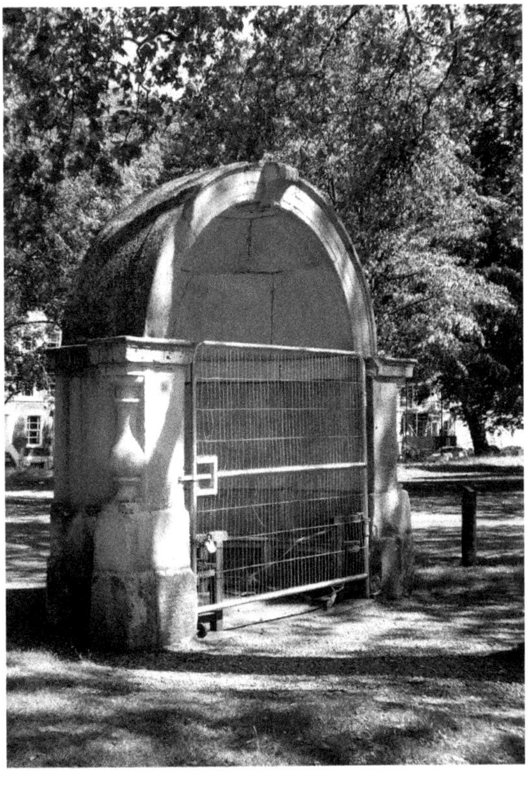

Right: Going back to Victoria Park, this is home to a pair of pedestrian alcoves that were once sited on the old London Bridge. This is the 1831 bridge by John Rennie that was replaced in 1973 and then dismantled and shipped out to Lake Havesu City, Arizona. When photographed in 2020 the alcoves were closed off to the public because of the coronavirus restrictions.

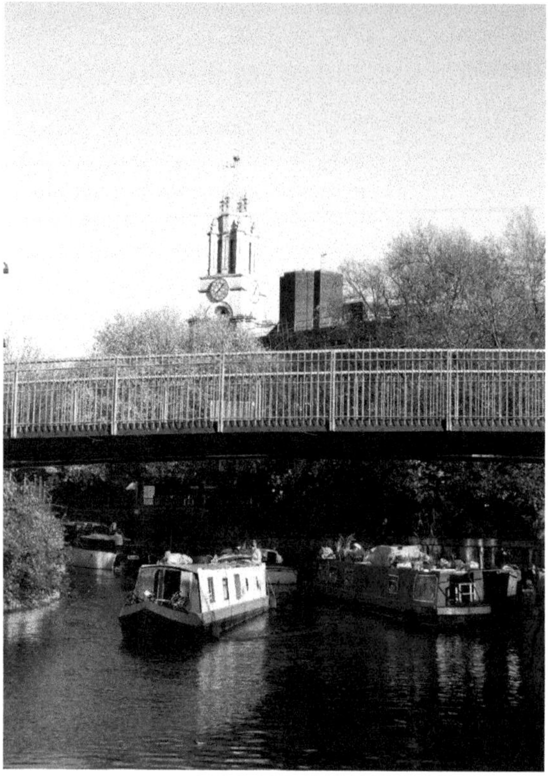

Left: Returning to Limehouse Basin, also leading off from here is the Limehouse Cut that connects to the River Lea at Bow Locks. This view is just beyond the Basin and the church is St Anne's, one of the three great Hawkesmoor churches in the East End. Begun in 1714, it was eventually consecrated in 1730.

Below: A view from about halfway along the Limehouse Cut, looking south-west towards Limehouse Basin.

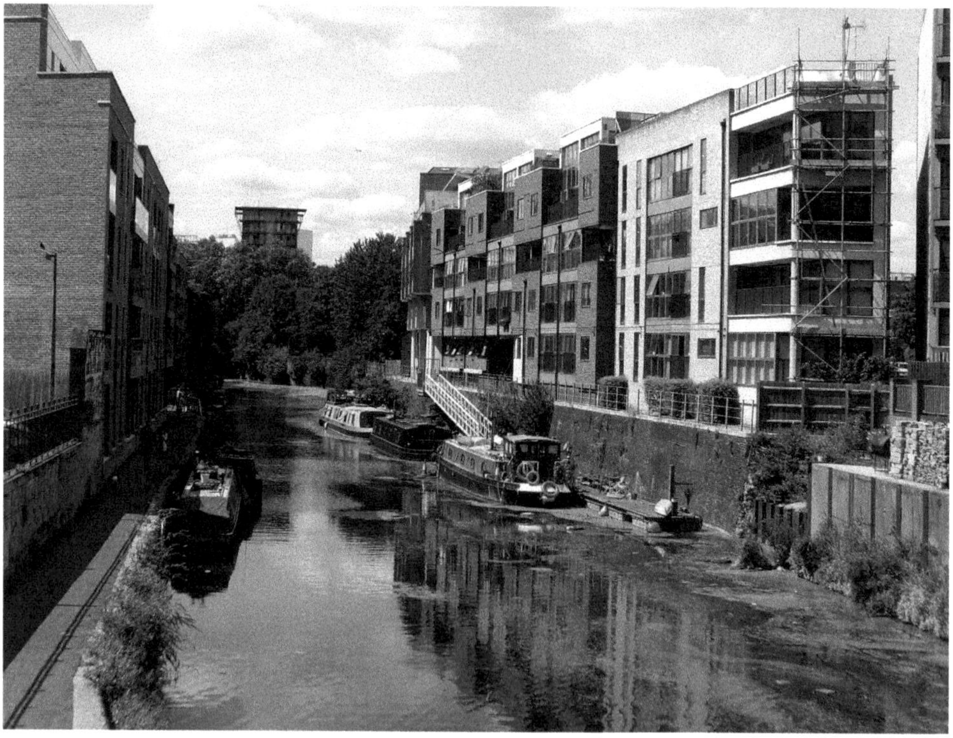

The Isle of Dogs at Island Gardens

The Thames Path on the north bank finishes at Island Gardens Park at the southern tip of the Isle of Dogs. It continues as the Thames Path Extension for another 2.5 miles to Trinity Buoy Wharf. This will be covered in the second volume along with the former West India and Millwall Docks that occupy much of the interior area of the Isle of Dogs.

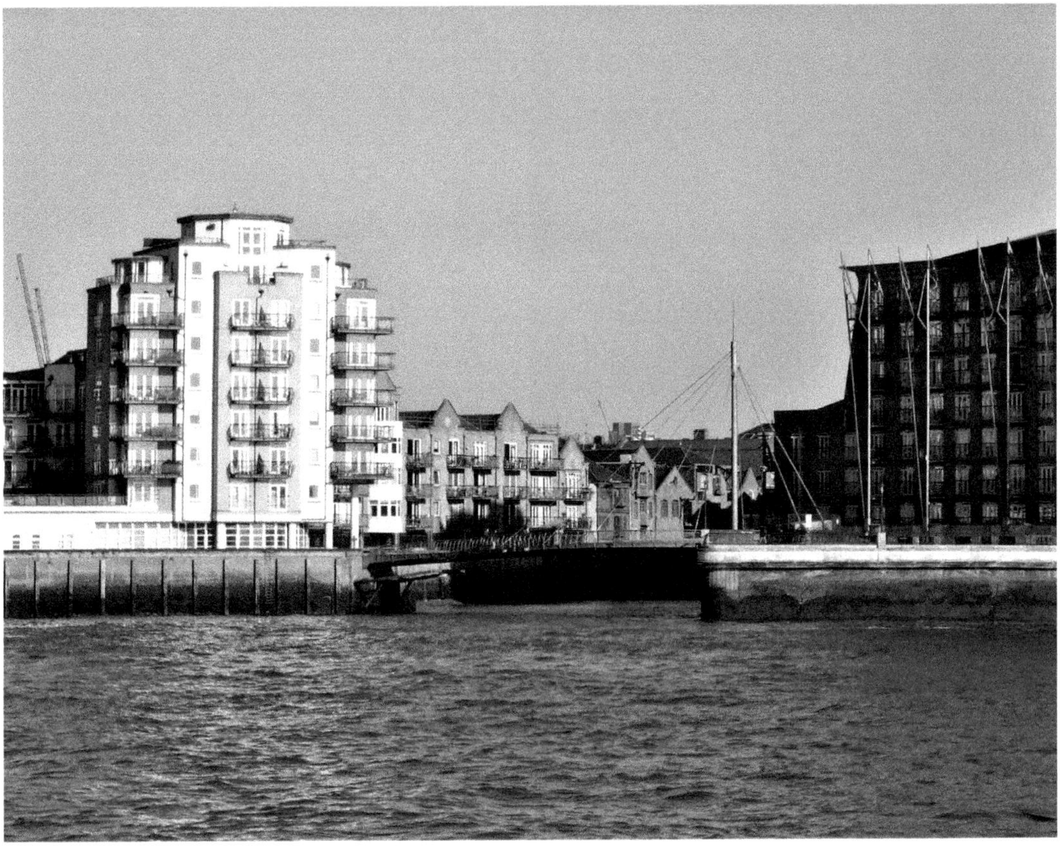

Much of the west riverside of the Isle of Dogs is occupied by modern blocks of flats in a variety of imaginative architectural styles. Just beyond the end of Narrow Street, however, an inlet to Dundee Wharf is spanned by a modern curved bridge. This is the entrance from the river and the bridge.

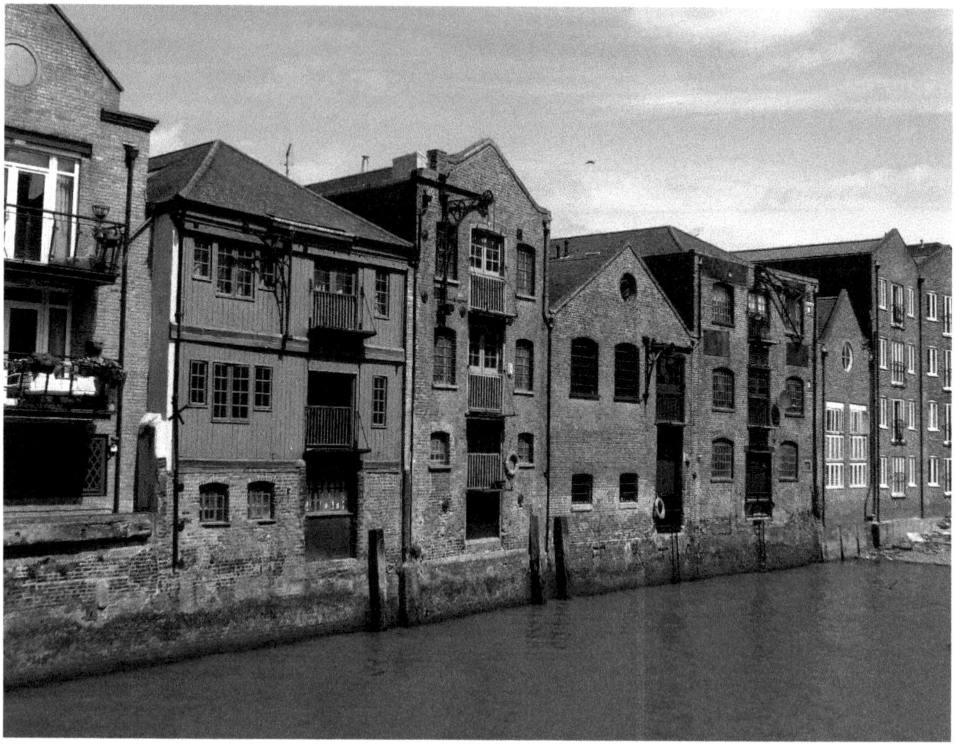

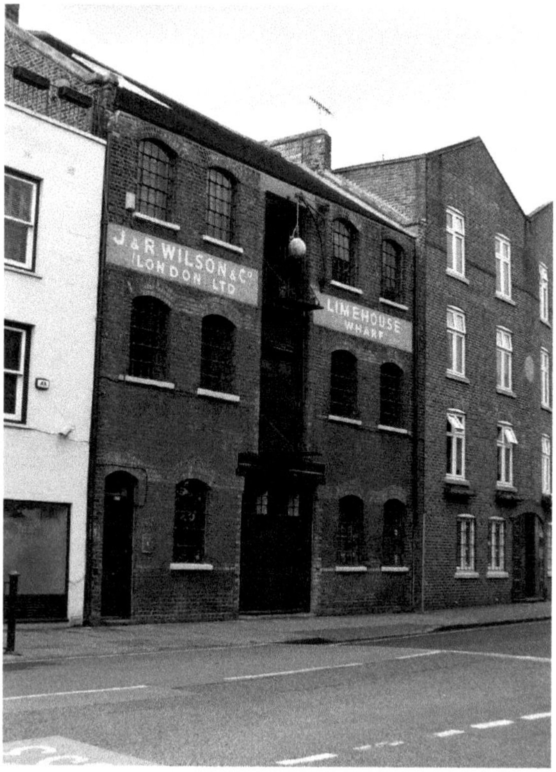

Above: A view along Dundee Wharf where some older former warehouses are juxtaposed with the modern flats. The wall-mounted cranes would have been used to load and unload cargo from lighters.

Left: One of the least changed of the warehouses is that of J. & R. Wilson & Co., seen from the landward side of Narrow Street.

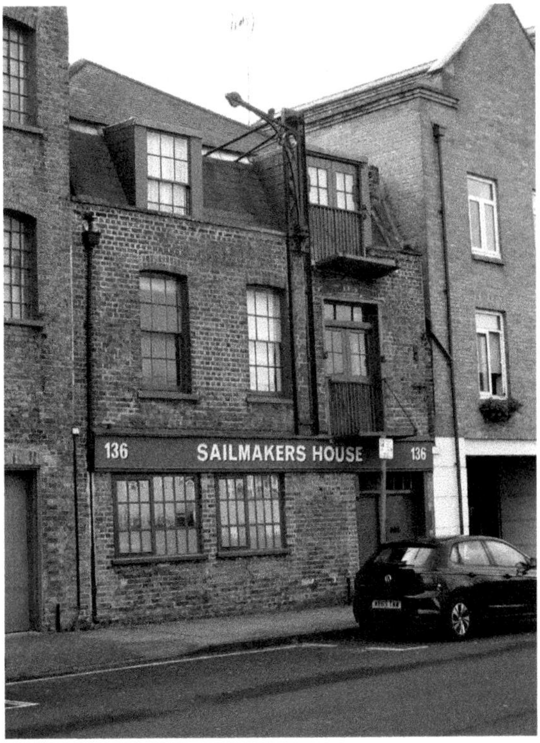

No. 136 Narrow Street is lettered Sailmakers House, a reminder of one of the marine crafts that used to be practised in this area.

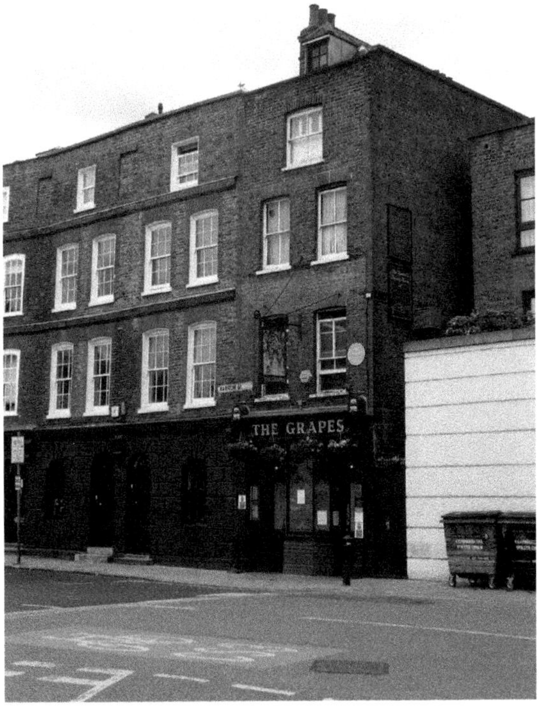

Nearby on Narrow Street, a row of Georgian buildings is ended by The Grapes. This ancient pub with a riverside terrace is now owned by the actor and local resident Sir Ian McKellan. Some think that this is the pub that Charles Dickens had in mind when, in his novel *Our Mutual Friend*, he described a pub called The Six Jolly Fellowship Porters.

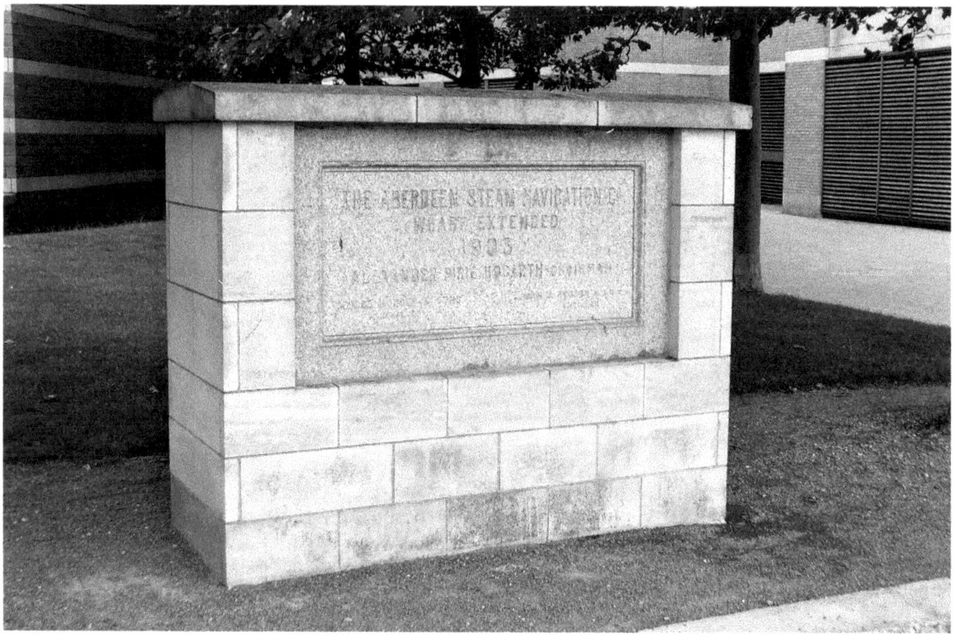

Moving onwards towards the modern Canary Wharf financial district, in Aberdeen Square is this monumental plaque. It reads 'The Aberdeen Steam Navigation Co. wharf extended 1903, Alexander Pirie Hogarth, Chairman'.

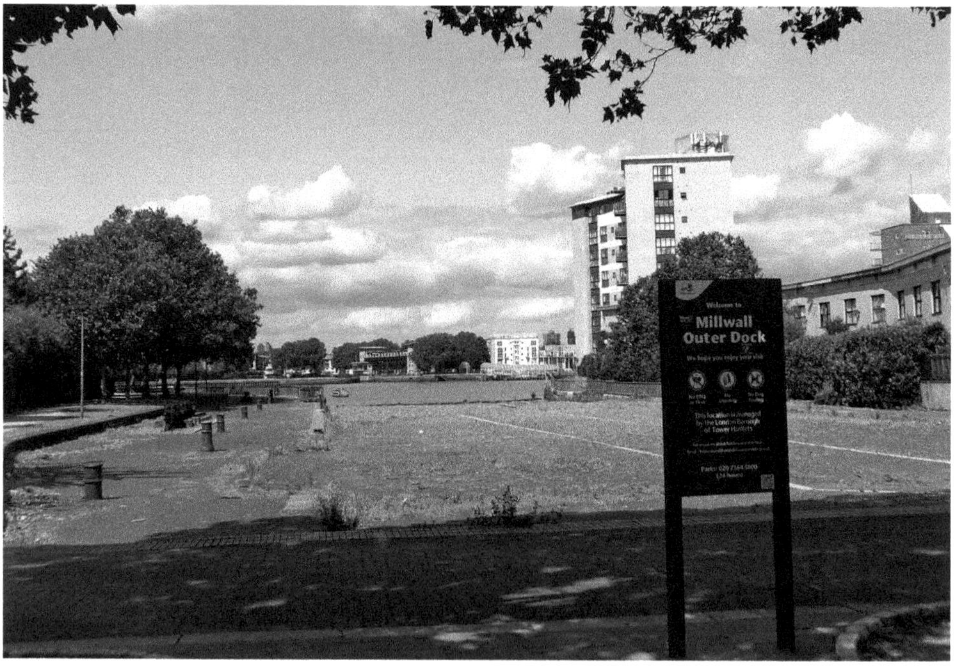

The Millwall Outer Dock formerly had an entrance lock at the western side of the Isle of Dogs, but this has been filled in. This shows the location of the former lock, looking towards the river. Millwall Dock opened in 1868.

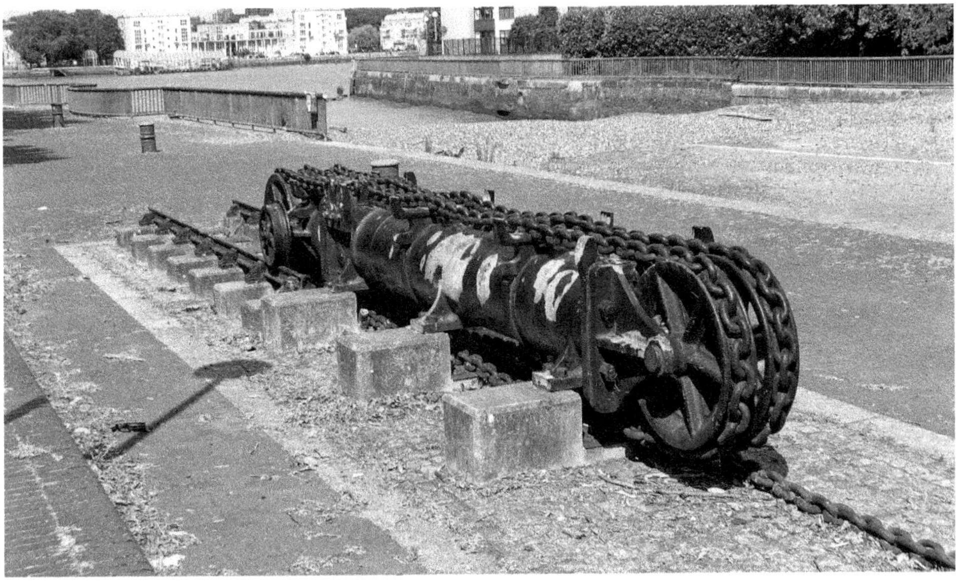

Part of the hydraulic mechanism to operate the lock gates preserved on site. The water pressure forced the piston up the tube, moving the wheels up the railway track to the left of the picture. This set the pulleys moving that pulled the chain at the far-right end, which in turn opened the lock gate. Across the river, the Shard can be seen in the distance, but vessels on the river will take a winding course before they reach London Bridge and the Shard.

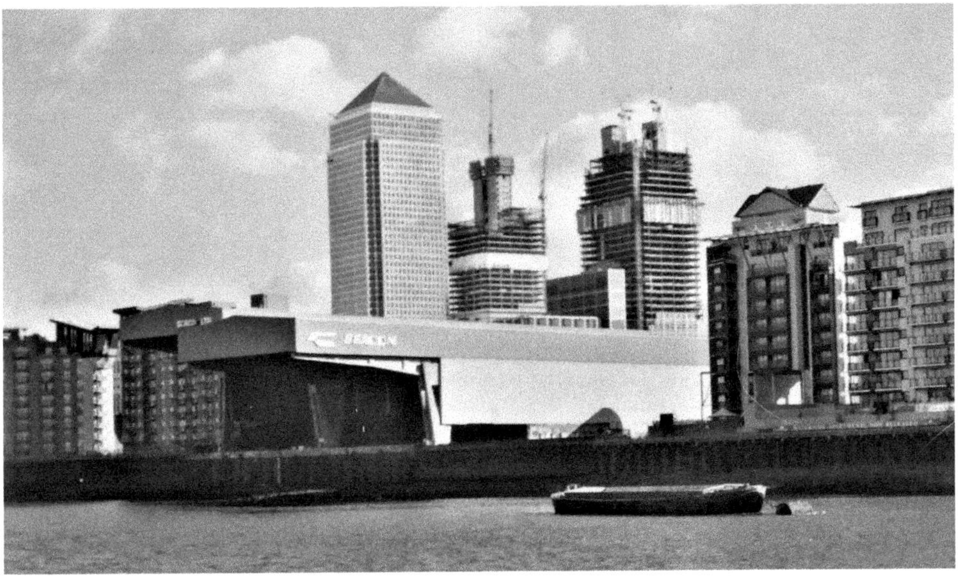

A view from the river taken back in 2000. The Canary Wharf district was still being developed at this time. The main Canary Wharf tower (One Canada Square) was complete but the other towers nearby are under construction. The Seacon terminal was still in place – a remaining vestige of the area's former maritime use. This had opened in 1976 to handle steel cargoes from the EEC. It would close by 2002 and be replaced by a new Seacon terminal at Northfleet near Gravesend. A twenty-one-storey housing block, Seacon Tower, now occupies the site.

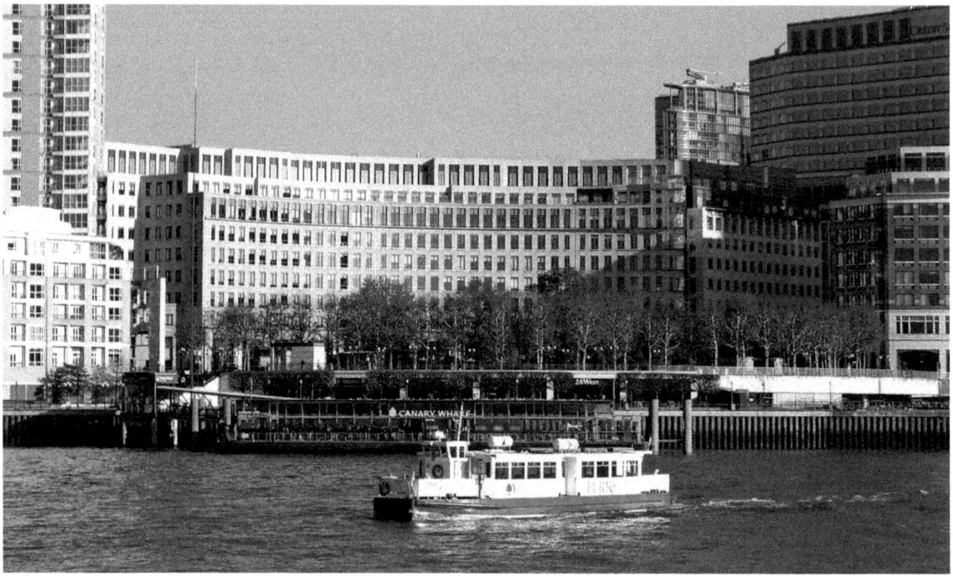

The Hilton Ferry links Canary Wharf Pier on the Isle of Dogs with Hilton Docklands Pier at Rotherhithe on the south bank since September 2004. This is run by Thames Clippers, who also operate the commuter ferries that link central London with various piers to Greenwich, the O2 Arena and occasionally Woolwich Arsenal Pier. It operates every 20 minutes (10 minutes at peak hours). An earlier service on this route had been operated by White Horse Ferries.

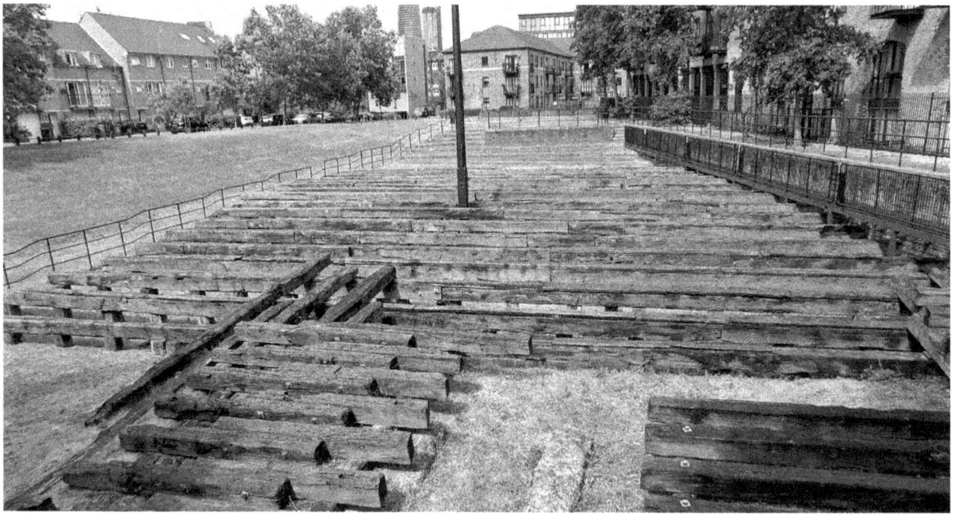

Just past Masthouse Terrace Pier at Burrells Wharf is this grassed area with rows of parallel timbers. This is the site where Isambard Kingdom Brunel's SS *Great Eastern* was launched in 1857. She was the largest ship in the world at the time at around 680 feet long and 12,000 tons deadweight and indeed held this record for the next forty years. She had paddle-wheels and a screw propeller, as well as six masts for sails. The first attempts at launching her were unsuccessful and several hydraulic jacks needed to be brought in before the launch was eventually completed. Because of her size, the ship was launched sideways for fear she might crash into the opposite bank with the momentum of the launch.

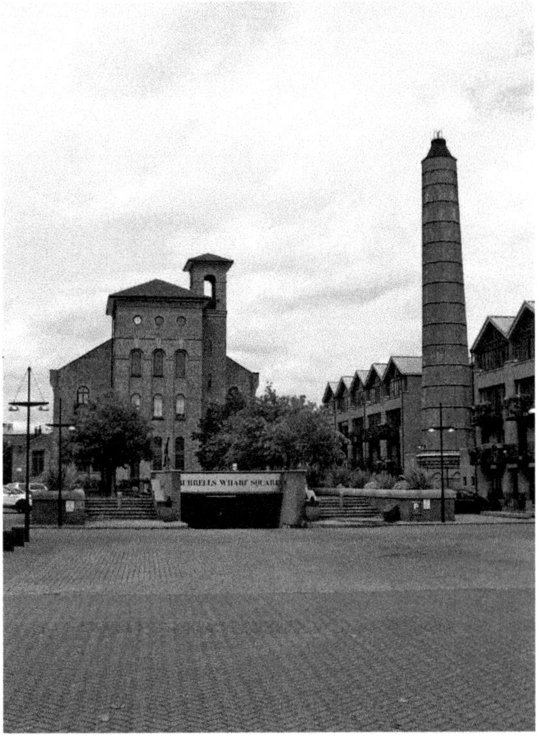

Burrells Wharf at the end of Napier Avenue. The shipyard was owned by J. Scott Russell & Co., who cooperated on the design of the *Great Eastern*. Although innovative in its size, its two-skinned metal hull and many other items, as a passenger carrying liner it was a financial disaster. After the delayed launch, Scott Russell went broke and Brunel also had financial problems. The ship was later employed to lay the first telegraph cable across the Atlantic, as it was the only one big enough to carry the quantity of cable for the job.

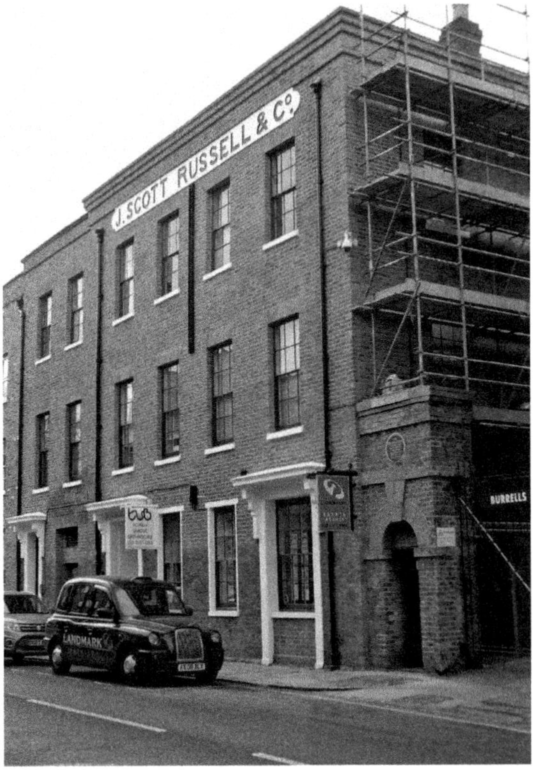

Nos 264–266 Westferry Road. This used to be the counting House of the shipbuilding firm J. Scott Russell & Co., whose name is still displayed on its frontage. The building now houses an estate agents and bathroom suppliers.

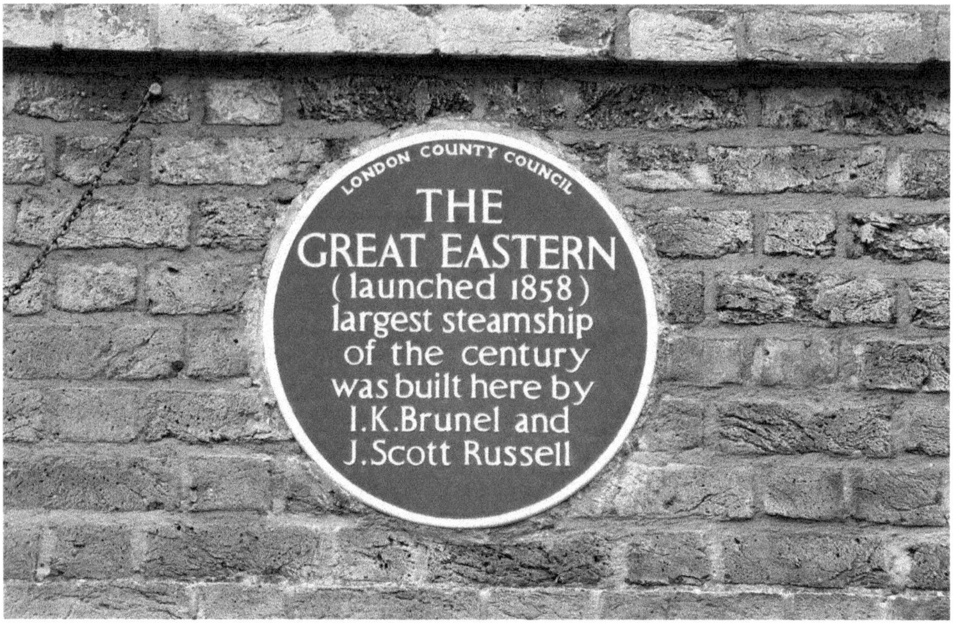

The blue plaque erected by the London County Council at the entrance to Burrells Wharf.

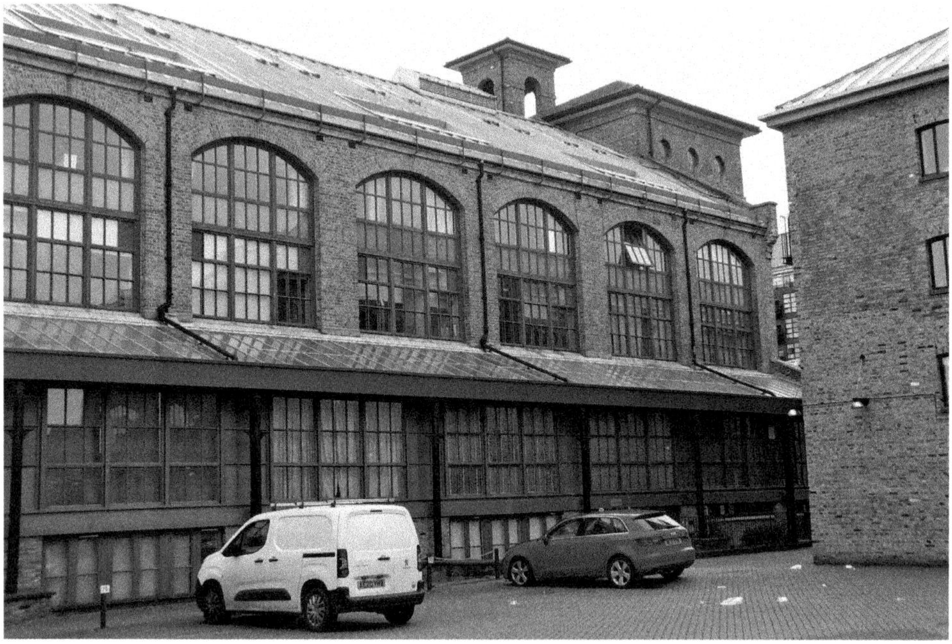

J. Scott Russell & Co.'s plate house in the middle of Burrells Wharf development, built by W. Cubitt & Co. It was here that the massive plates for the hull of the *Great Eastern* and other ships were manufactured. They were moved about by overhead cranes on gantries. After Scott Russell went out of business, the site was taken over by Napier's, hence the name Napier Avenue. The building has now been converted to apartments with an internal swimming pool. Some of the internal iron beams are still visible.

Right: At the southern tip of the Isle of Dogs is Island Gardens, and here is the northern entrance to the foot tunnel under the river to Greenwich. Before the Docklands Light Railway was extended under the river to Lewisham in 1999 this was the only means of crossing here. The tunnel is 390 metres long, with eighty-eight steps down at Island Gardens and 100 steps at Greenwich (there are also lifts). It was built in 1902. Island Gardens was laid out in 1895 by the Naval College in Greenwich to improve the view from the south bank, a scrapyard having occupied the site before then.

Below: From Island Gardens, the classic view across to Greenwich. The former Royal Naval College is a World Heritage site. Queen Anne's house is the white building seen between the two towers. Greenwich observatory is on the hilltop in the distance.

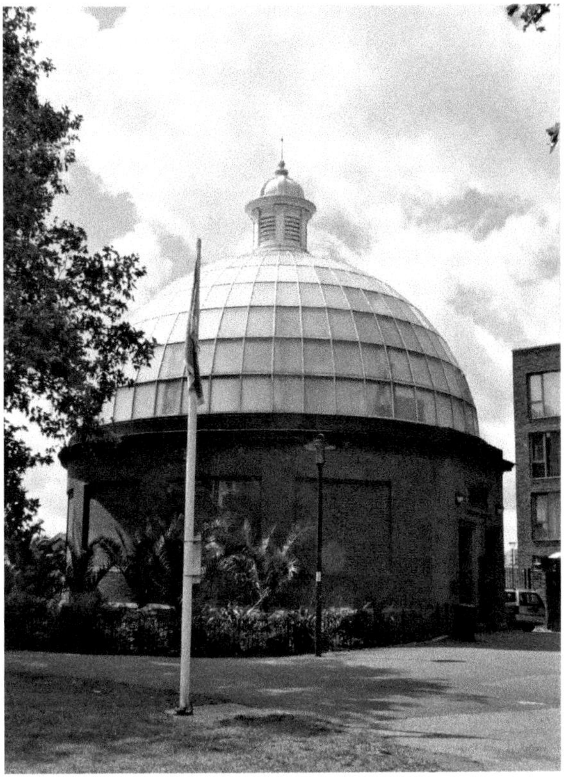

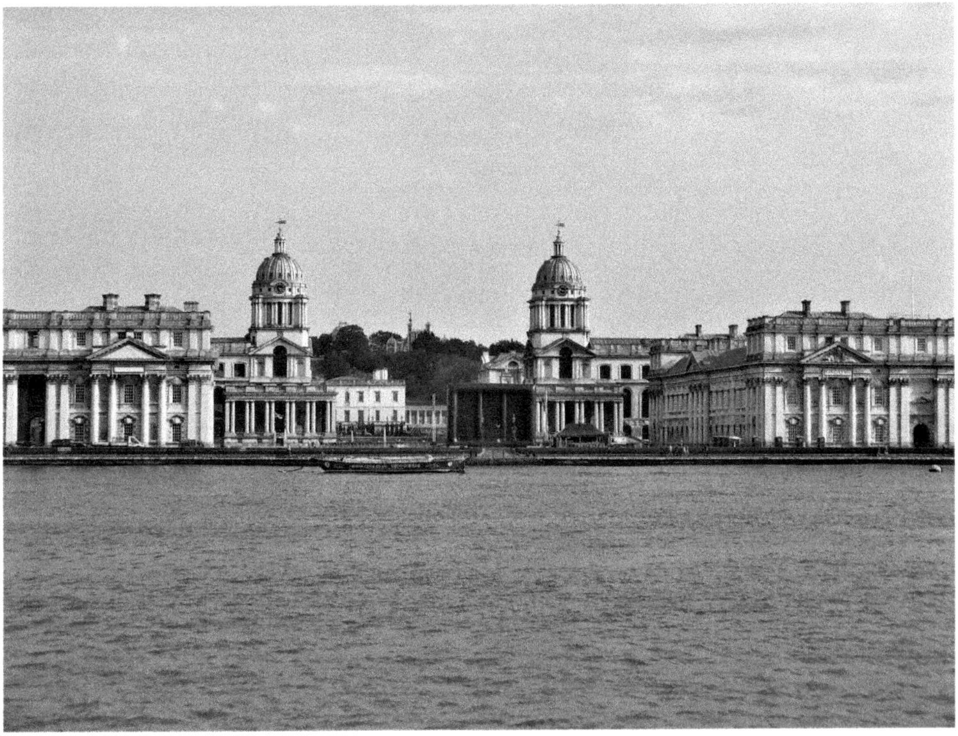

SOUTH BANK – LONDON BRIDGE TO GREENWICH

London Bridge to Rotherhithe

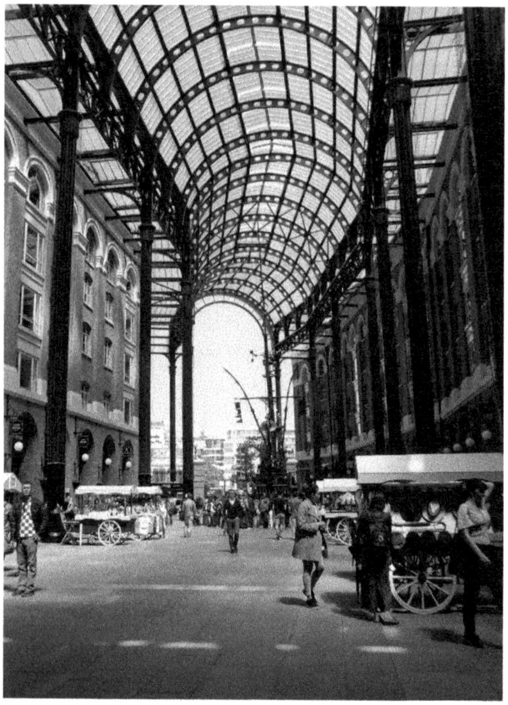

Left: Hays Galleria. Hays Wharf was a centre for importing tea and later dairy produce before the advent of containerisation and the closing of the Upper Pool. It was rebuilt as Hays Galleria in 1988 with shops, stalls and restaurants. The surrounding area has been redeveloped under the collective name of London Bridge City.

Below: Two of London's most iconic modern buildings: the London City Hall building designed by Norman Foster and opened in July 2002, and the seventy-two-storey Shard by Renzo Piano, completed in 2012. In March 2022 the London Assembly moved to the Crystal building, a site in Newham alongside the Emirates Air Line at Royal Victoria Dock'.

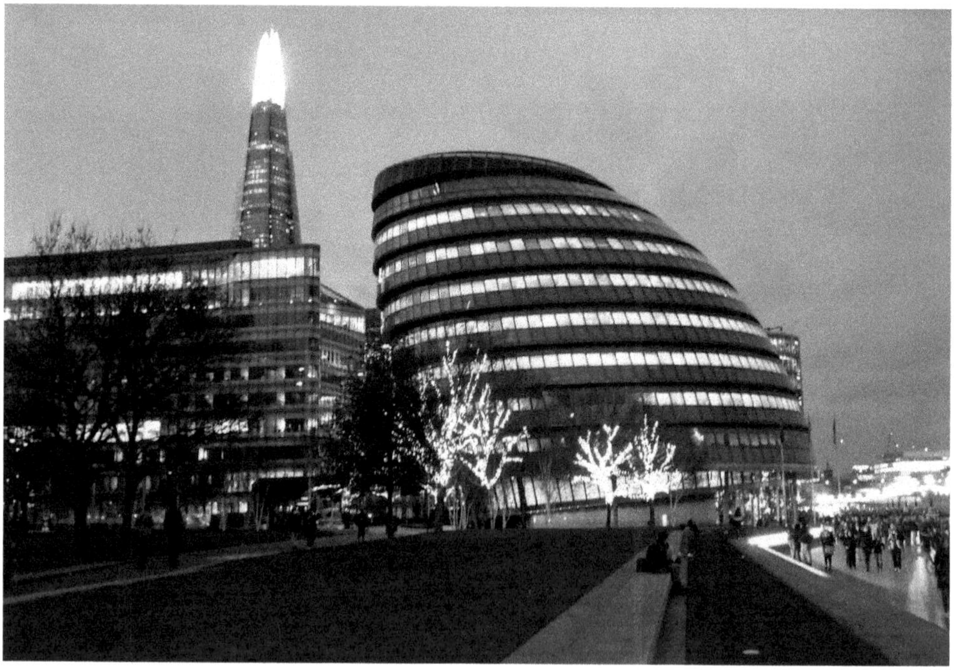

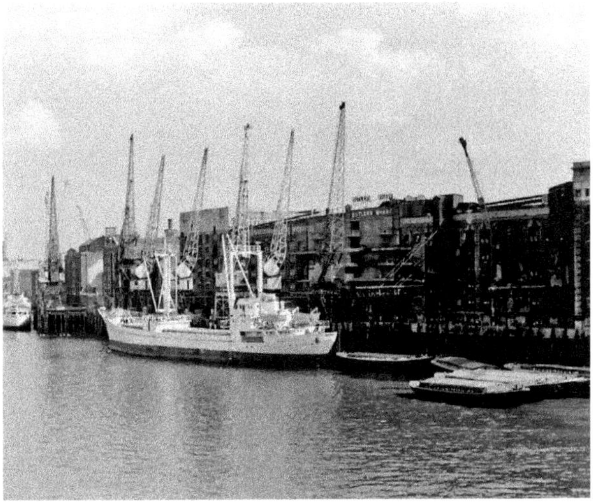

Butlers Wharf lies just to the east of Tower Bridge in the Lower Pool. This view is from the 1950s, when this area was still part of the active Port of London. (Reg Batten)

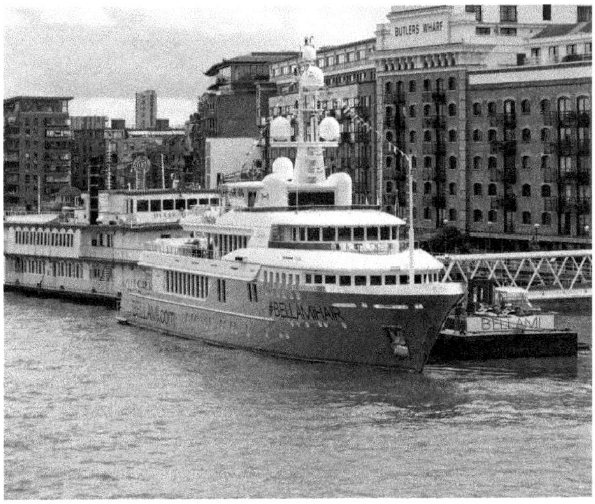

Butlers Wharf in 2019. The wharf buildings remain, but in use for shops, restaurants, etc. Where once commercial shipping traded, there are moorings for some of the rivercraft that provide evening party trips such as the *Dixie Queen*, a mock Mississippi-style stern paddler. The gold and white 'superyacht' was on some sort of promotion for haircare products.

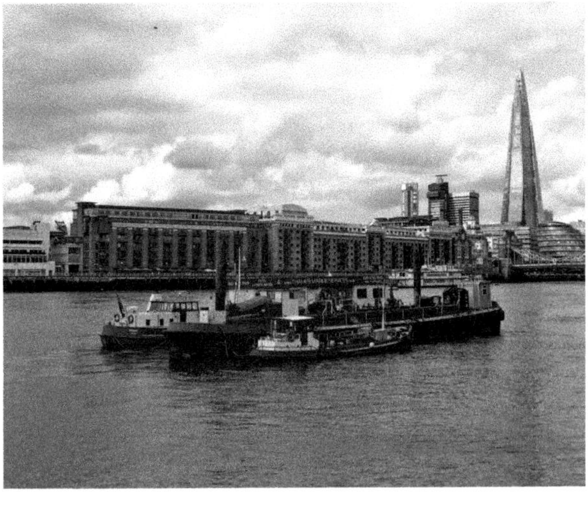

A view of Butlers Wharf from the north bank, with Tower Bridge, the London Assembly building and the Shard to the right. The white building on the extreme left was formerly the Design Museum but this has since moved to Kensington. At the other end, nearest Tower Bridge, is Courage's former Anchor Brewery, which closed in 1982. Thames Marine Services provide bunkering for the various pleasurecraft on the river.

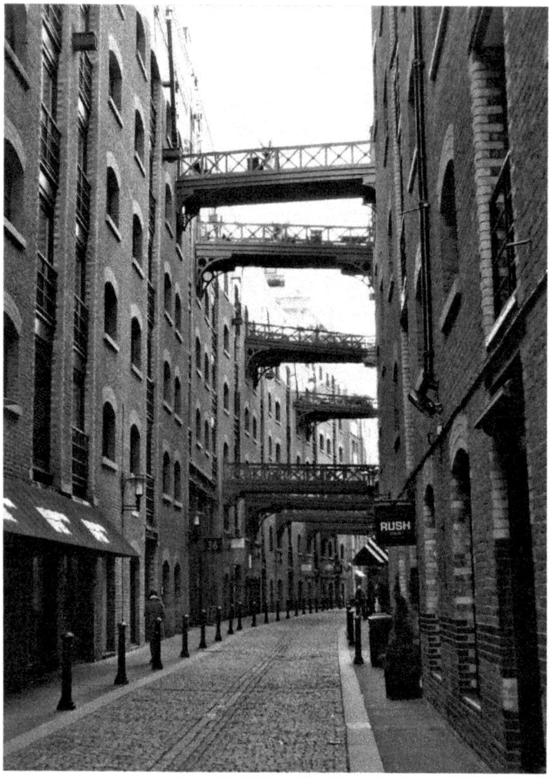

Left: Shad Thames, behind Butlers Wharf, is a narrow road where warehouses were linked by overhead walkways. These remain but the road is now a trendy tourist area of shops and eateries. To appreciate the old atmosphere, it is best photographed, as here, early on a Sunday morning.

Below: Beyond Butlers Wharf is the deep inlet of St Saviour's Dock, named after a Cluniac abbey that once stood here. The former warehouses have again been turned into flats. The river entrance is spanned by a modern footbridge from which this view is taken.

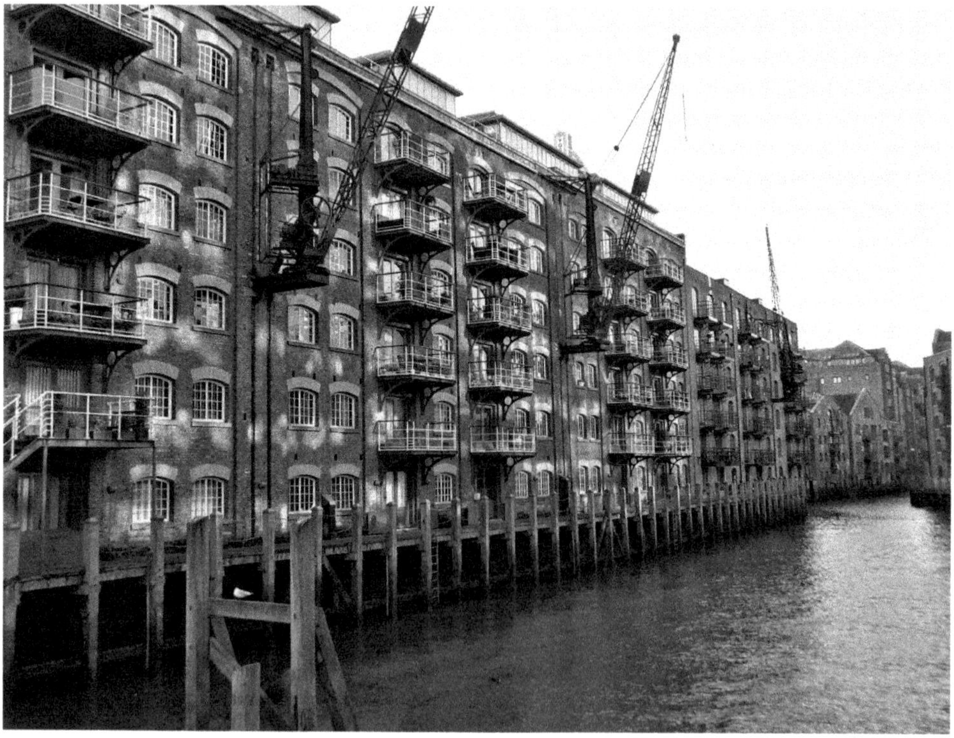

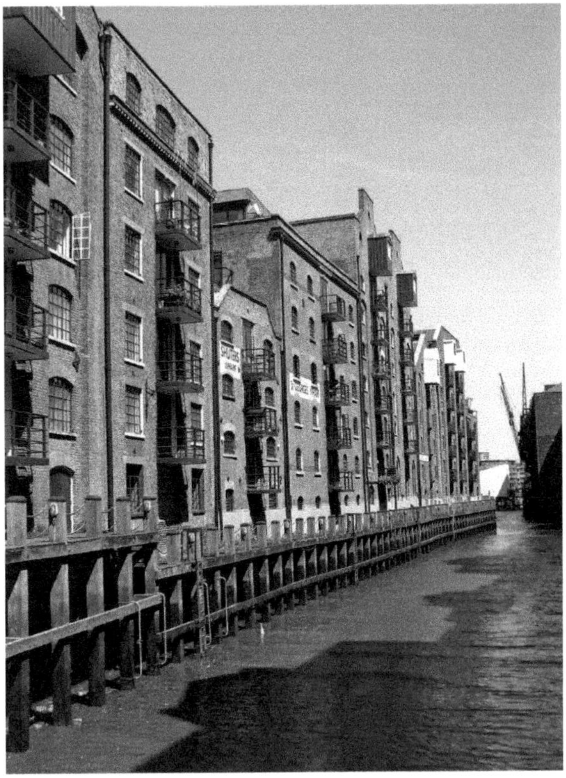

Right: The other side of St Saviour's Dock, seen from the landward end where it extends down as far as Dockhead, at the junction of Tooley Street and Jamaica Road. This is the mouth of the River Neckinger, so named after the 'Devil's Neckinger', London slang for the noose used to execute pirates who used to rob ships moored here before the docks were built.

Below: On the other side of the entrance to St Saviour's Dock are Downings Roads moorings for several houseboats. A Thames barge can also be seen. On the north bank are some of the converted wharves we saw earlier. In the distance, the towers of Canary Wharf are ever present.

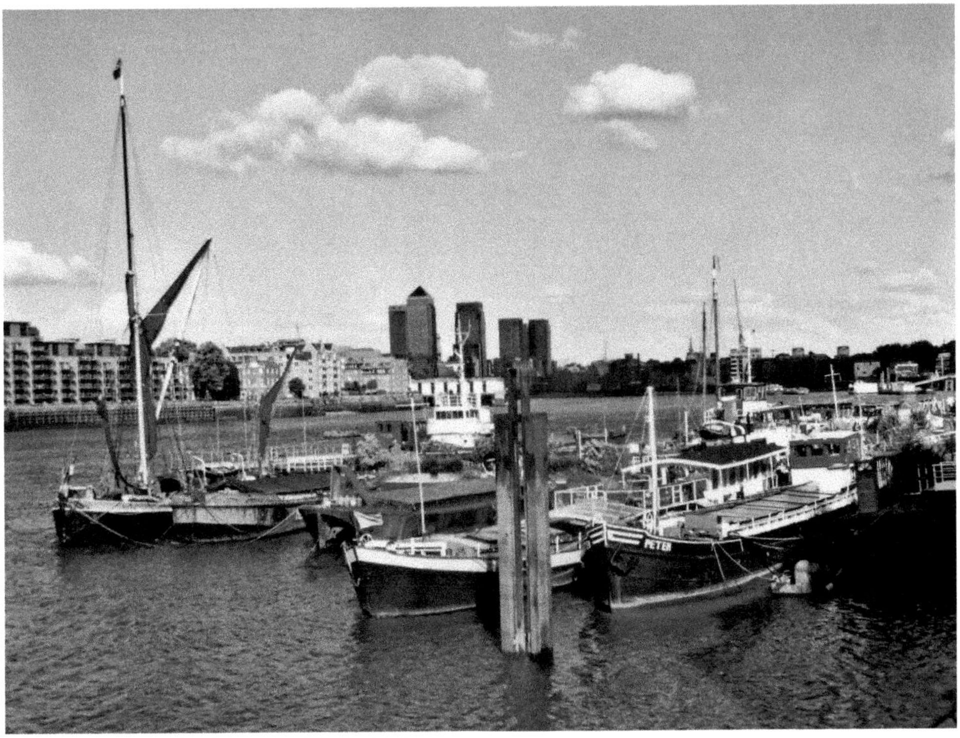

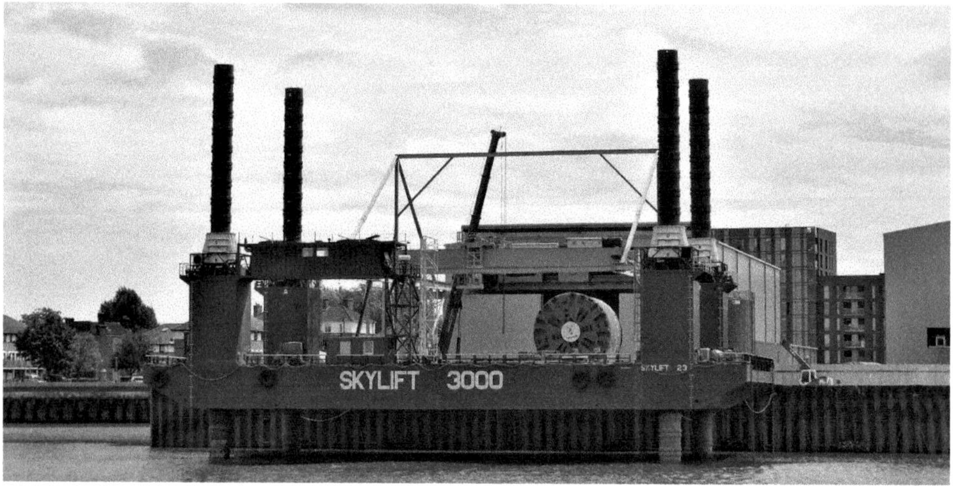

Chambers Wharf, Bermondsey, has become one of the main drive sites for the Thames Tideway project, meaning that it will be used to launch the tunnel boring machine (TBM) *Selina,* which will travel 5 km eastwards to Abbey Mills Pumping Station. It will also receive *Ursula* the TBM from their central site and *Annie* the TBM, used to form the Greenwich connection tunnel. On 13 July 2020 the semi-submersible *Skylift 3000* has brought one of the TBMs to the site for offloading. It was a complicated job to bring this upriver, which had to be managed at the correct height of the tide because of the limited clearance under the Emirates Air Line cable car at Greenwich.

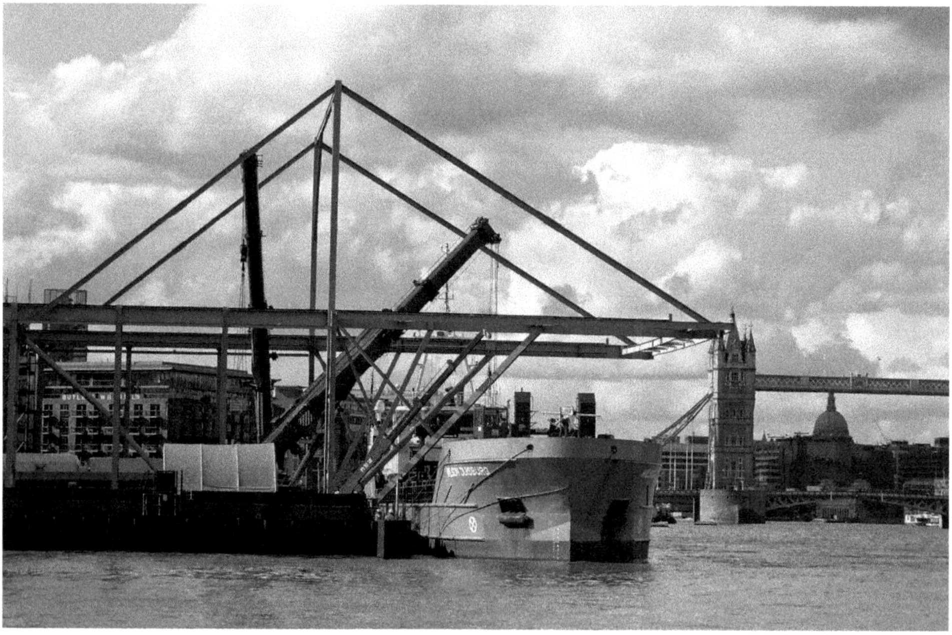

On 1 October 2020 the coaster *Wilson Duisburg* is seen unloading at Chambers Wharf. This had arrived the previous evening. It is very rare these days for such a vessel to travel this far upriver as there are no other commercially operating wharves now beyond Greenwich except for aggregates and domestic containerised refuse.

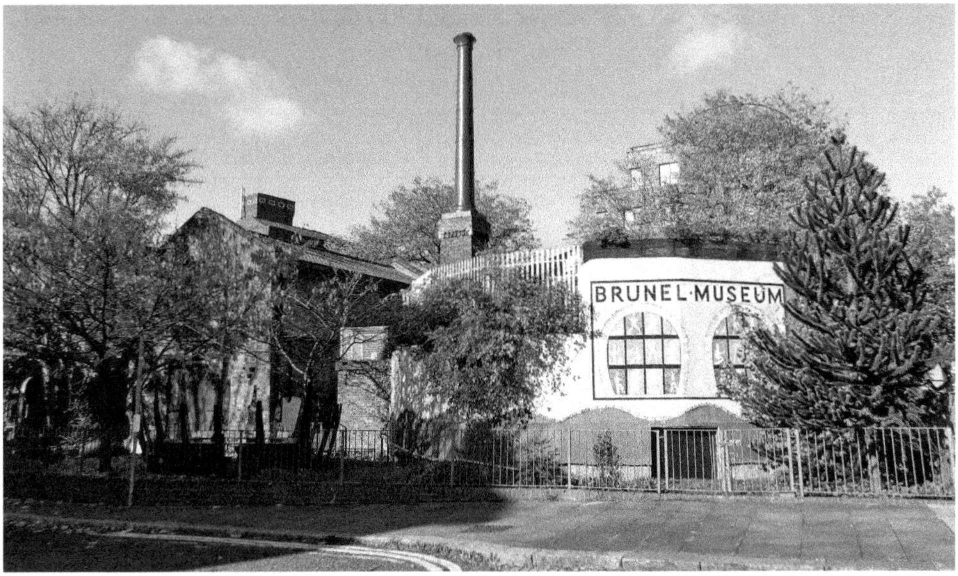

The Brunel Museum at Rotherhithe, located in the engine house built to pump water from the first Thames tunnel built by Marc Brunel and incorporates the tunnel shaft. Isambard Kingdom Brunel worked on the project with his father, being appointed Resident Engineer in 1827 at the age of twenty. Flooding caused problems during building and a serious breach in January 1828 nearly cost Isambard his life.

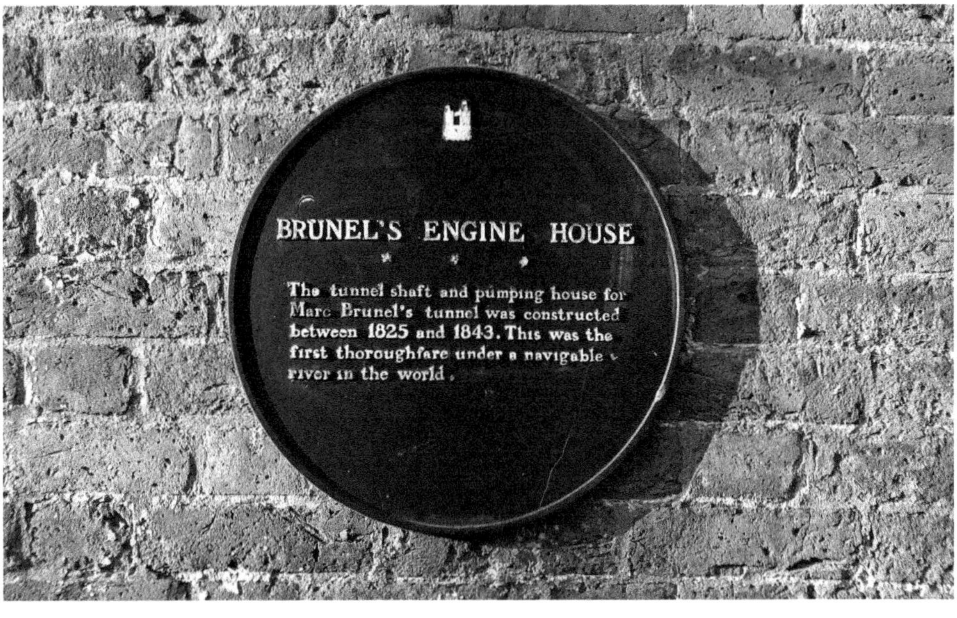

A plaque mounted on the wall of the engine house. The text reads 'The tunnel shaft and pumping house for Marc Brunel's tunnel was constructed between 1825 and 1843. This was the first throughfare under a navigable river in the world'. It was constructed using an early form of tunnelling shield in which the tunnellers dug out a section of tunnel, then lined it and jacked the shield forward.

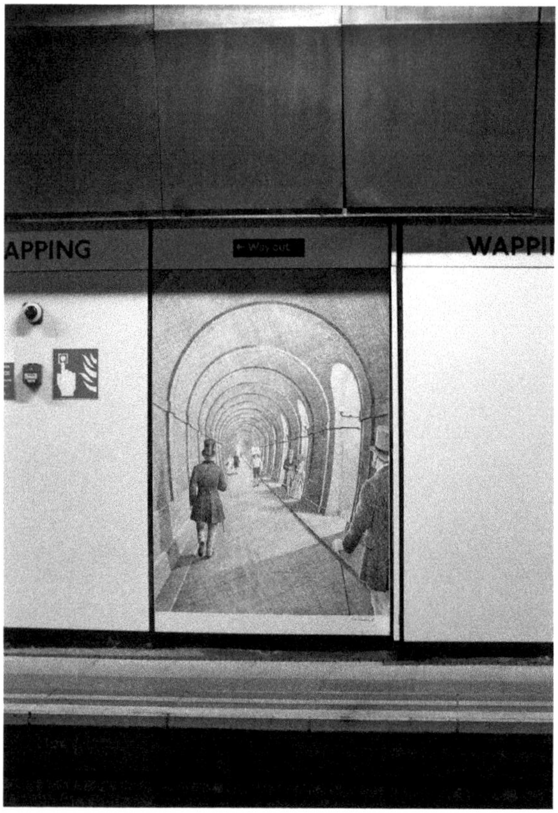

Left: Brunel's tunnel became a railway tunnel and this became part of the London Underground East London Line from Shoreditch (at certain times) and Whitechapel to New Cross or New Cross Gate. In December 2007 this closed for rebuilding, during which the line has been extended to become part of the London Overground linking Highbury & Islington to West Croydon, Crystal Palace and Clapham Junction. The first stage reopened in May 2010.Wapping station has murals showing the history of the tunnel including its early days as a foot tunnel.

Below: Another of the murals shows an Underground train and also a freight train. There was a connection (now removed) from Shoreditch to the Great Eastern main line into Liverpool Street so trains could access this route to get south of the river, although they would have to reverse at Liverpool Street.

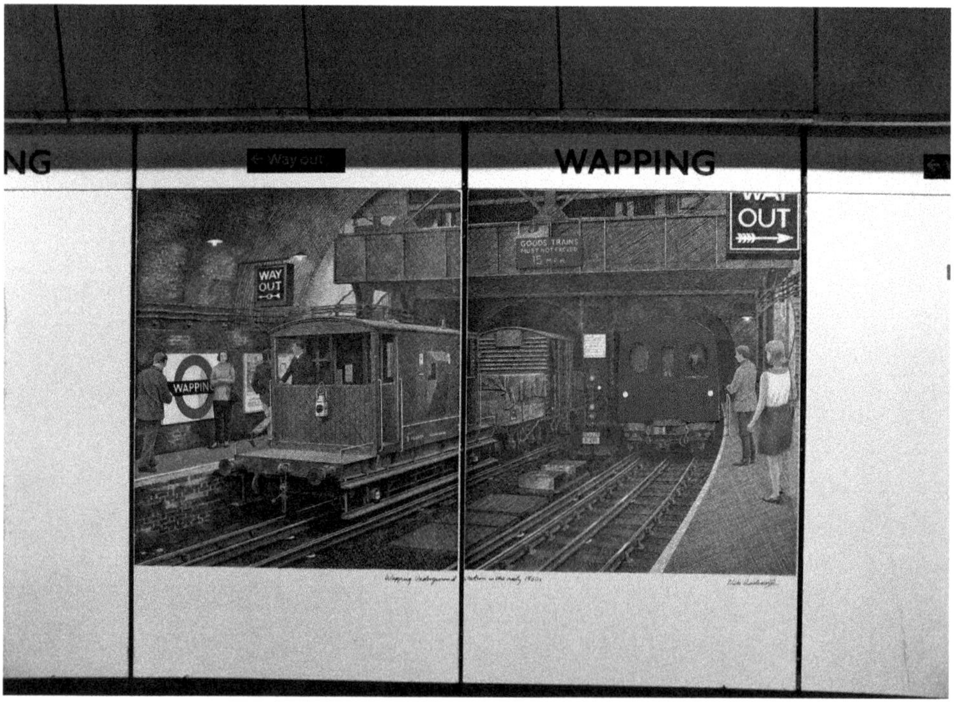

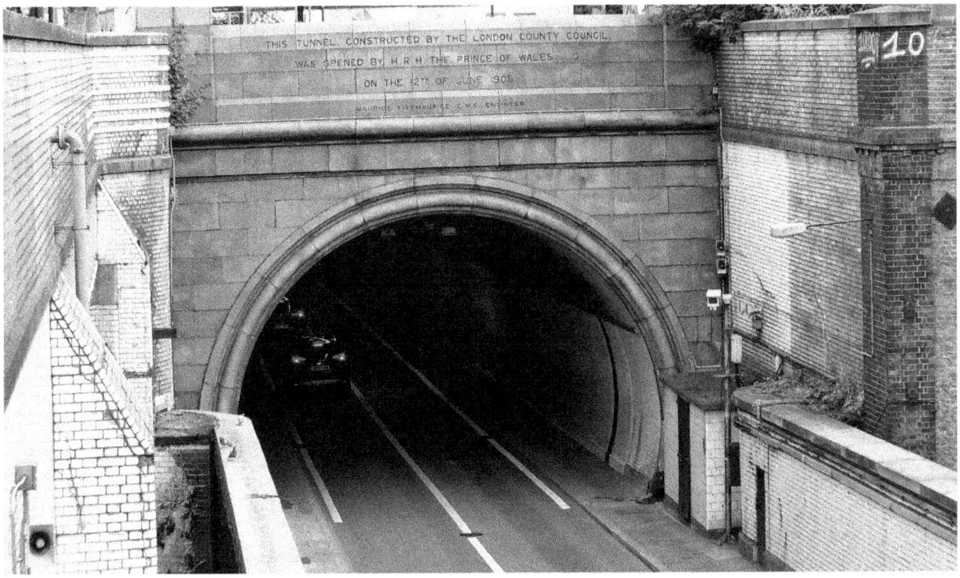

Although Tower Bridge remained the most easterly bridge until the Queen Elizabeth II Bridge at Dartford opened in October 1991. Two road tunnels were constructed in east London in the early twentieth century. The Rotherhithe tunnel was constructed by the London County Council and opened on 12 June 1908 by HRH The Prince of Wales, so states the inscription above the southern entrance. The engineer was Maurice Fitzmaurice.

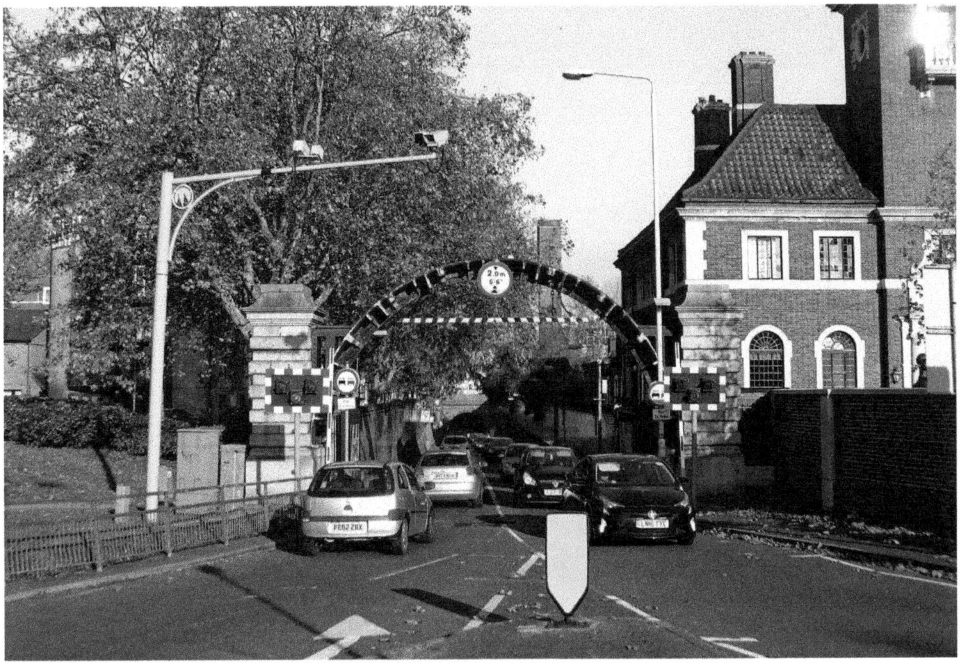

The southern entrance to the Rotherhithe tunnel. The tunnel is narrow and twisting. Although it formerly had double-deck buses running through it, no buses run through now and there is a height restriction of 2 metres (6 feet 6 inches) limiting it to cars and vans.

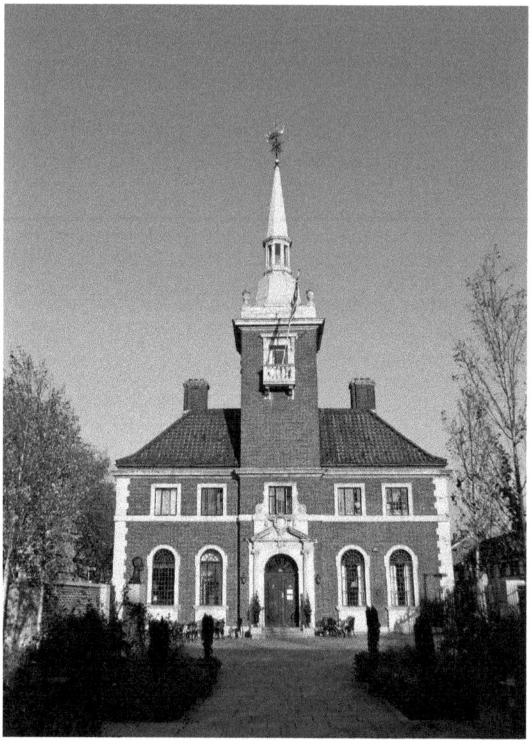

By the entrance to the Rotherhithe tunnel is the Norwegian church. The nearby Surrey Docks was the main discharging point for timber traffic, much of it coming from Scandinavian countries, so there would be many seamen from Norway, Sweden, the Baltic states and also Russia lodging in the area.

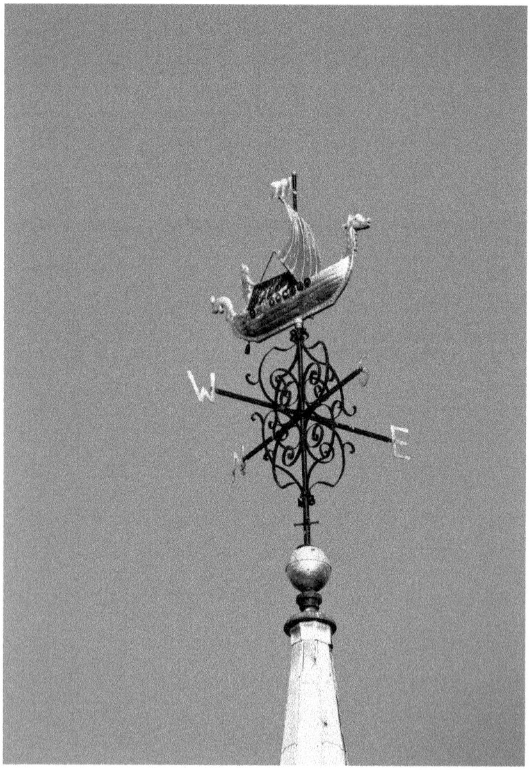

The weathervane of the Norwegian church features a Viking galley.

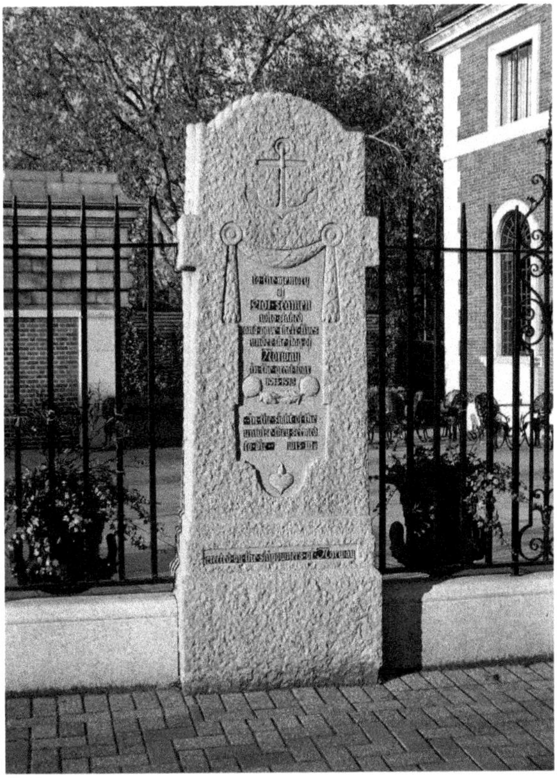

Right: Outside the church is a war memorial. The inscription reads 'To the memory of 2101 seaman who staked and gave their lives under the flag of Norway in the great war 1914–1918'.

Below: The remains of a disused pier and beyond that the southern Rotherhithe tunnel access and ventilation shaft. This would have been the access point when the tunnel was open to pedestrians but is now just an emergency exit.

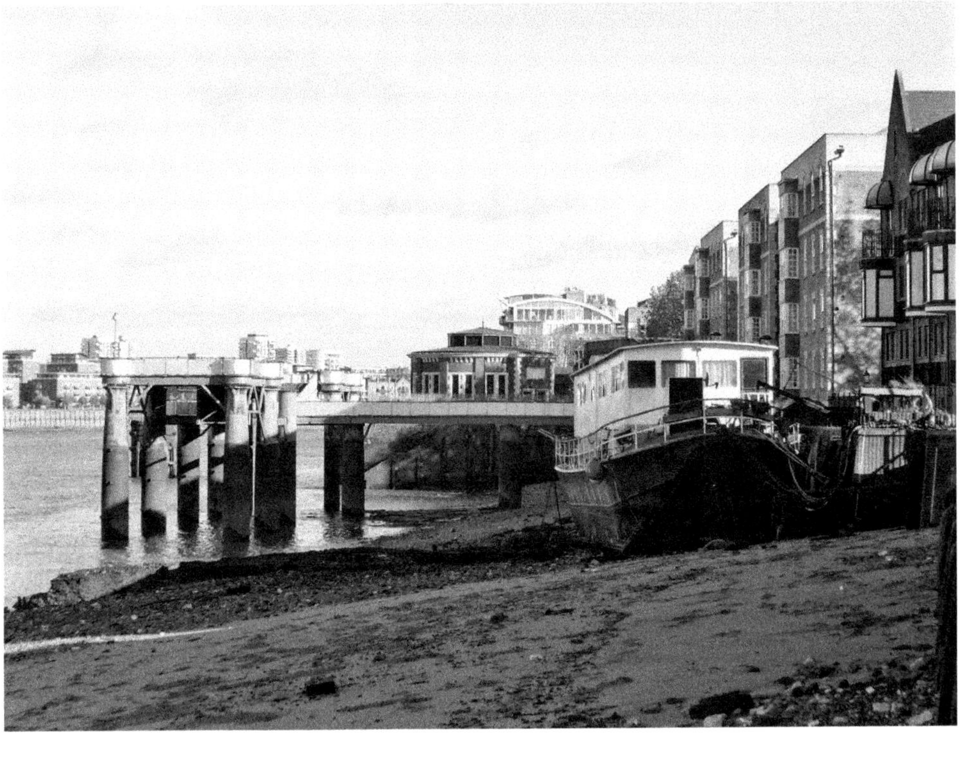

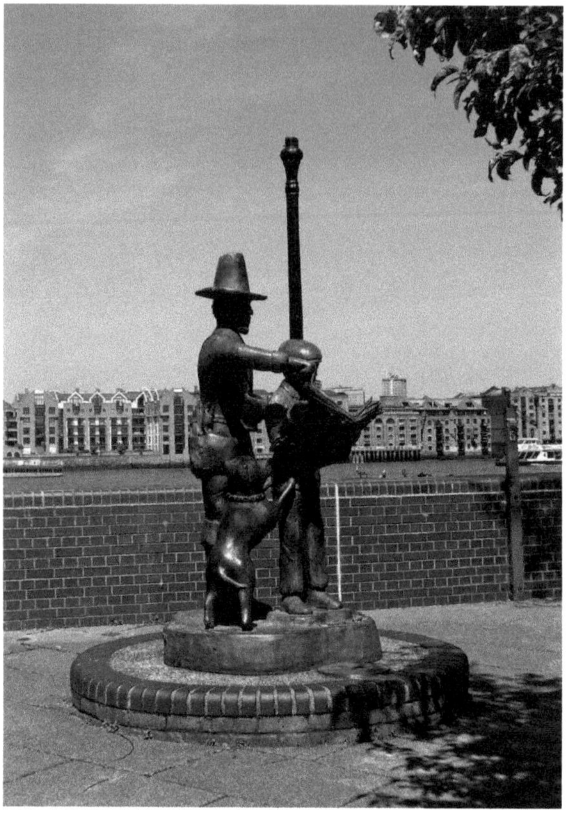

Left: At Cumberland Wharf, Rotherhithe, is a statue to the Pilgrim Fathers.

Below: An explanatory display erected by Southwark Council states that Cumberland Wharf was the approximate site from where the *Mayflower* first set off with the Pilgrim Fathers on their voyage to find a new home in America. They stopped off for supplies in Southampton and Plymouth from where they set sail across the Atlantic Ocean on 6 September 1620.

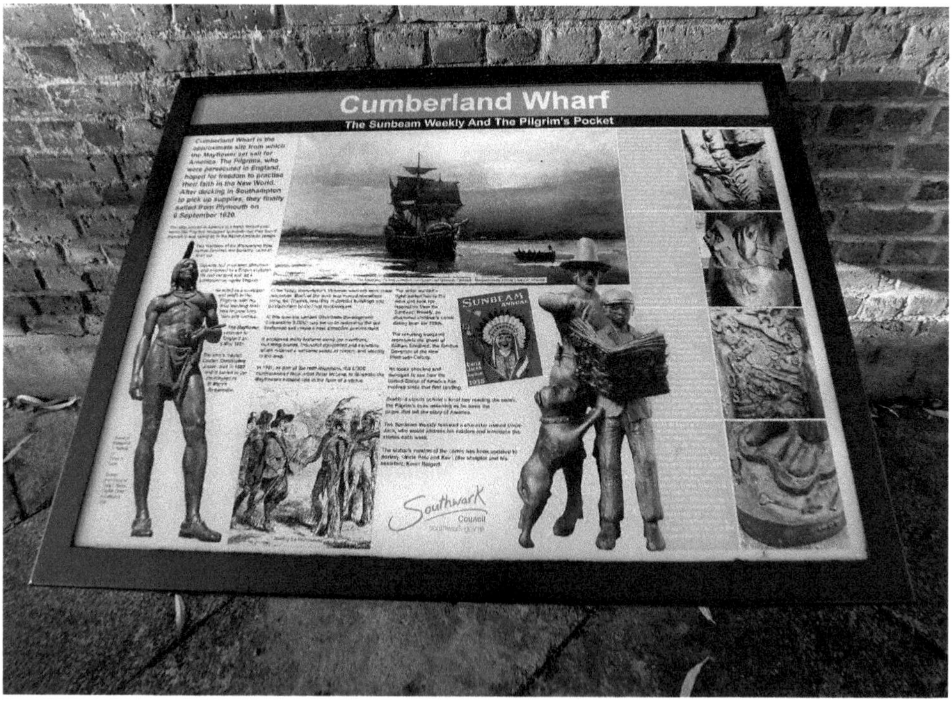

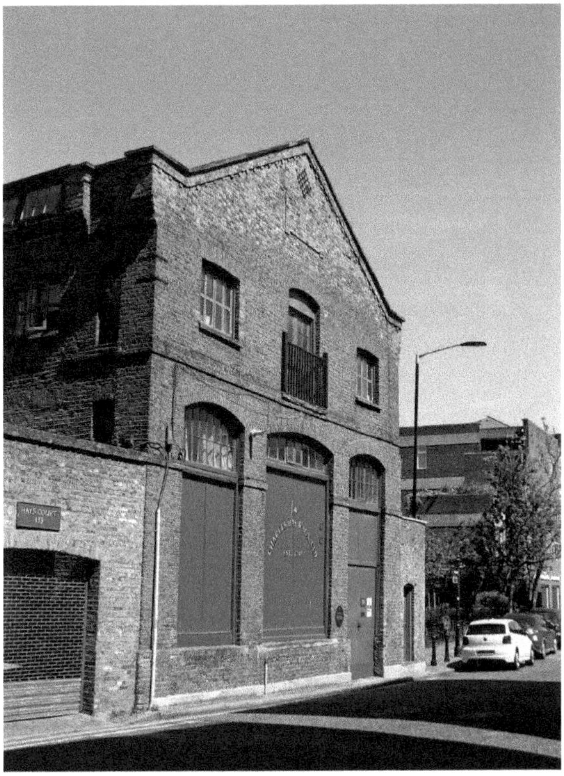

Right: Nearby at No. 135 Rotherhithe Street is the premises of Charles Hay & Sons barge builders and ship repairers.

Below: A plaque on the building reads: 'This listed mid-nineteenth century building has been occupied by Charles Hay & Sons established since 1789. It is one of the few surviving barge building and repair workshops on the Thames'.

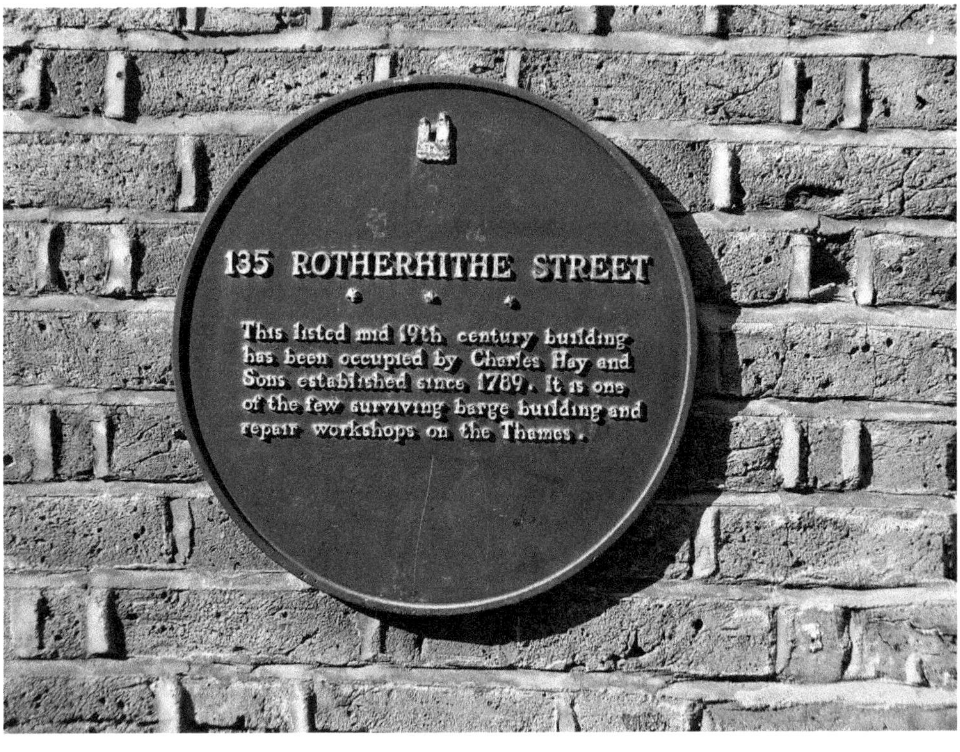

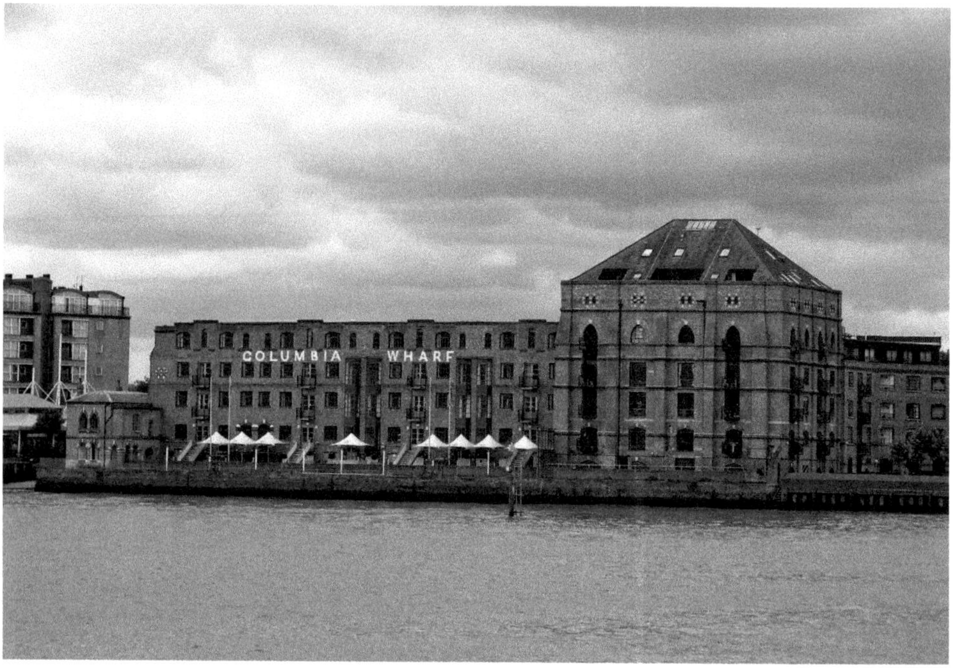

Rounding the top of the Rotherhithe bend and moving into Limehouse Reach we come to Columbia Wharf, seen from across the river. Again, this has been converted into flats.

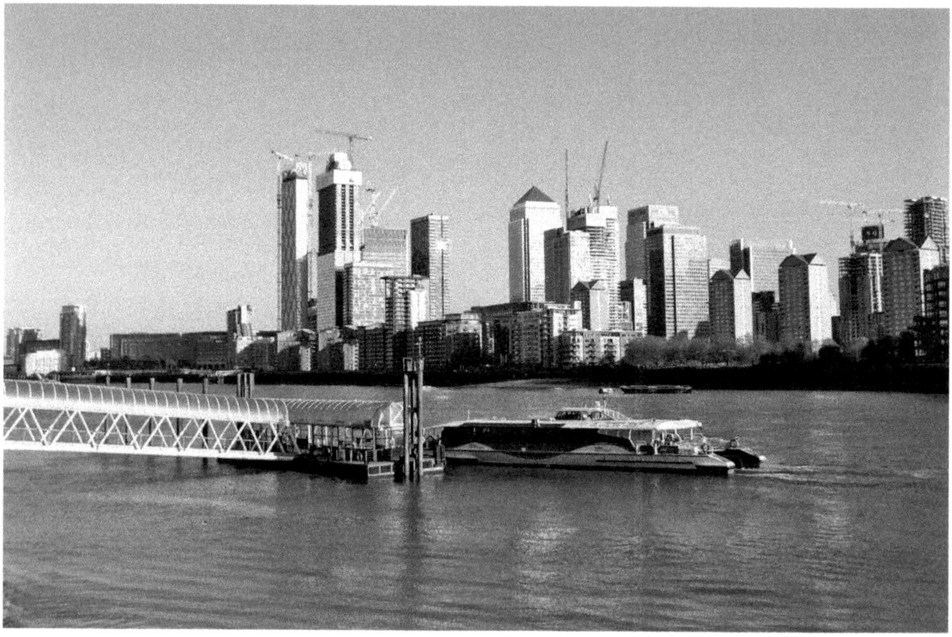

One of the Thames Clipper commuter ferries arrives at Greenland Pier, one of the new piers constructed for the service. This is at the entrance to the former Surrey Docks. Across the river is the Isle of Dogs and the number of cranes in this 2018 view shows that development was (and is) still continuing apace.

Surrey Docks

Surrey Docks were the only part of London's Docks on the south side of the river and were largely associated with the timber trade. Since closure in the 1970s some of the dock areas have been filled in while others remain. The area has been redeveloped mainly for housing and retail use. Many artefacts from the former docks have been preserved with explanatory plaques and display boards provided by Southwark Council.

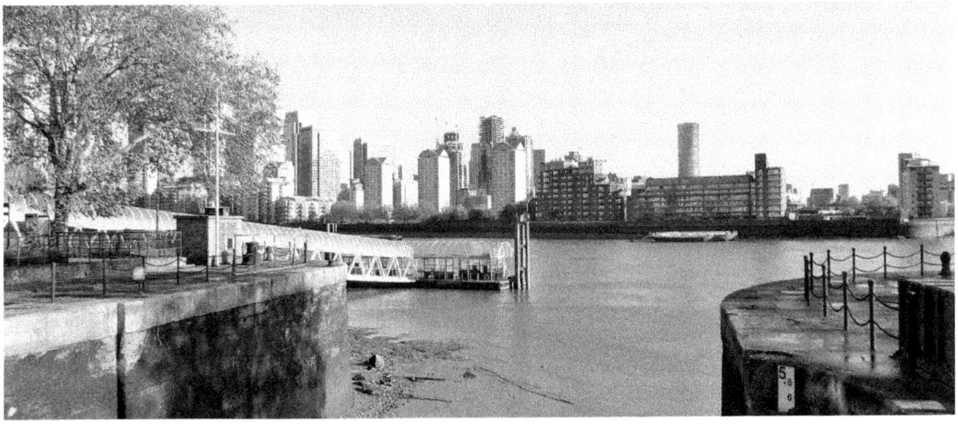

Greenland Pier is adjacent to the lock entrances to Surrey Docks. This is the South Lock, which gave entry to South Dock. Beyond the pier lies Greenland Lock, the former entrance to Greenland Dock.

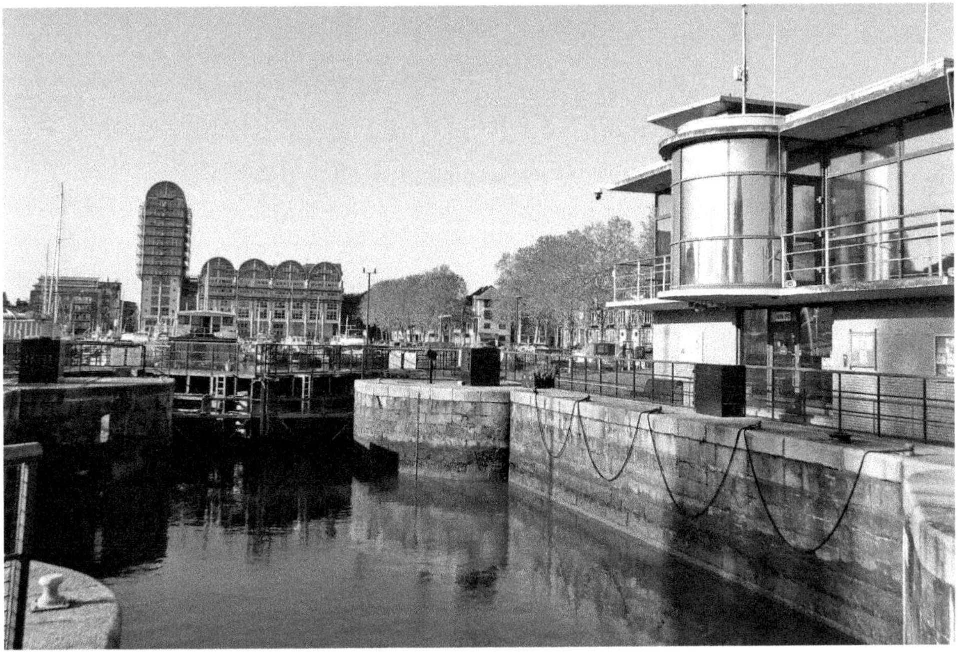

The South Dock lock remains operational as this is now the entrance to a marina.

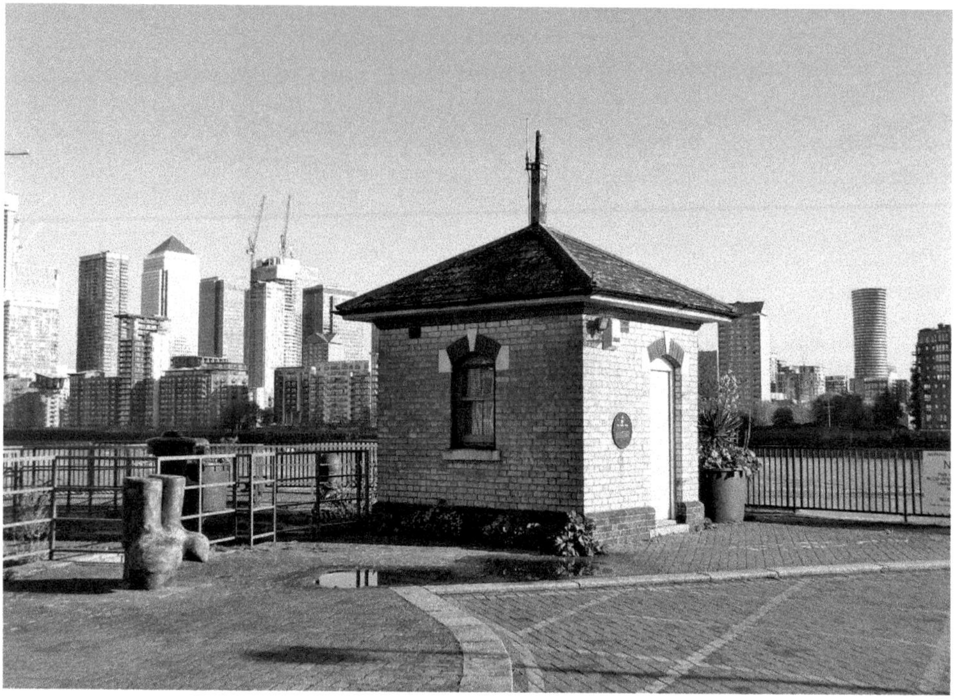

By the lock entrance is the tide gauge house.

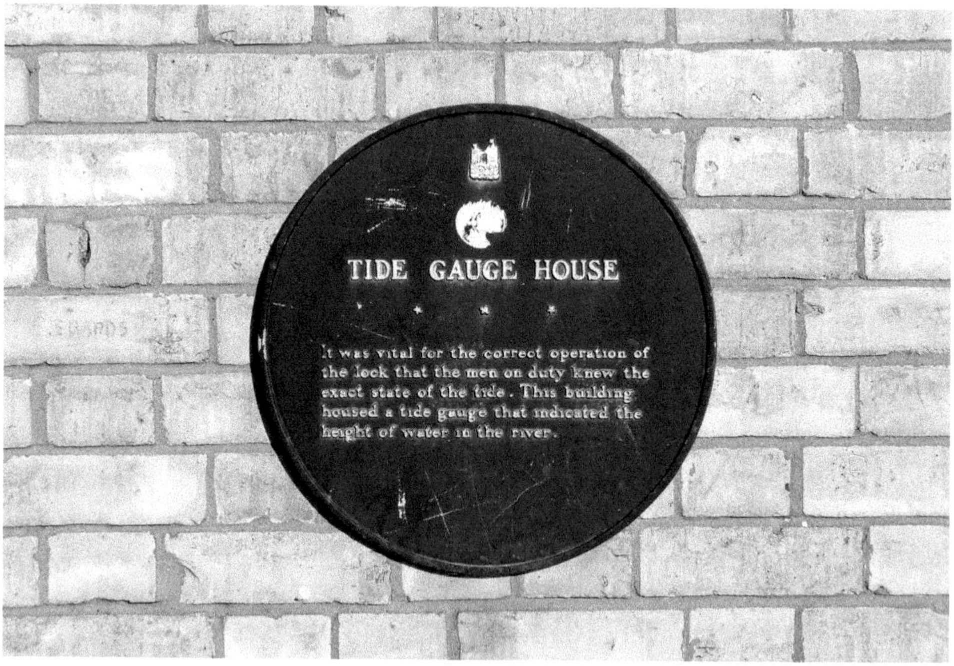

The tide gauge house has a plaque that reads: 'It was vital for the correct operation of the lock that the men on duty knew the exact state of the tide. This building housed a tide gauge that indicated the height of water in the river'.

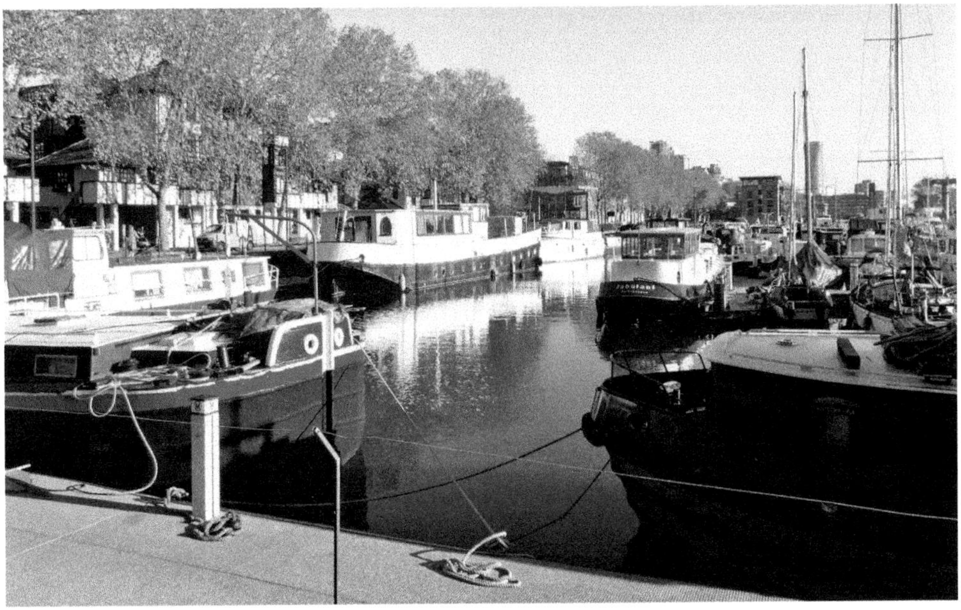

South Dock and Greenland Dock are now a marina. Greenland Dock is the oldest part of the dock system, having been originally the Howland Great Dock first built in 1695–9 for the whaling fleet. It was renamed in 1793. The dock was much enlarged between 1895 and 1904 at a cost of £940,000.

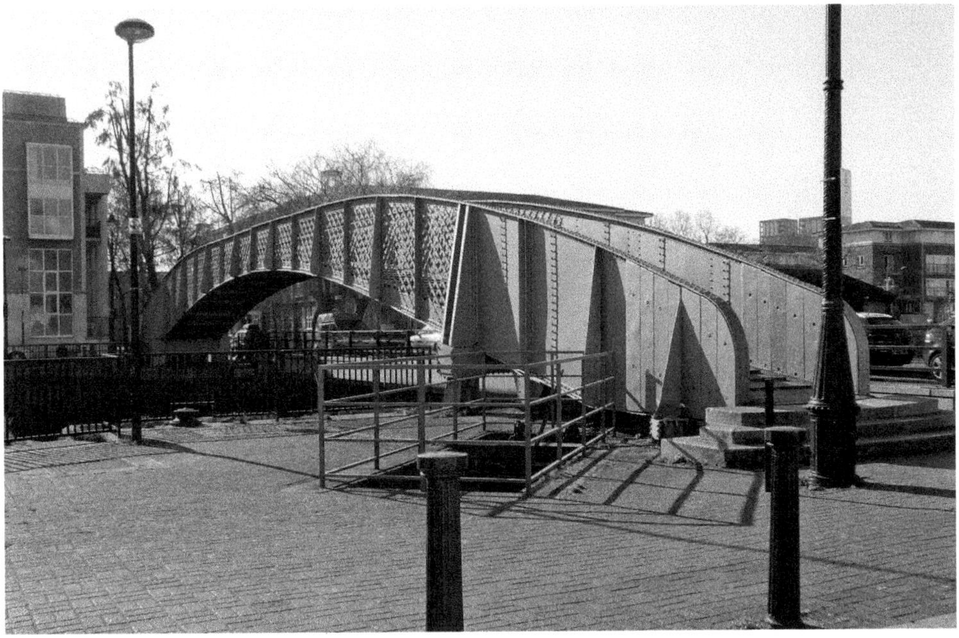

The preserved 1902 hydraulic swing bridge over the lock at the entrance to Greenland Dock in Rotherhithe. The jiggers to operate the nearest swinging span are in the pit by the lamppost. The road bridge to the right of the swing bridge has been installed since closure of the lock to shipping and is non-opening.

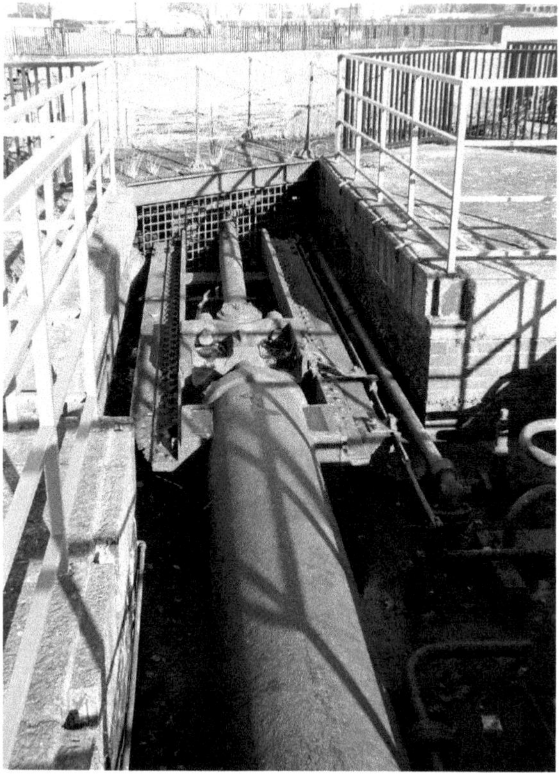

Left: Some of the preserved hydraulic mechanisms that variously operated the swing bridge, lock gates and sluices at the entrance to Greenland Dock.

Below: There are various artefacts from the former working dock system such as this footbridge at Norway Cut. The two sections swivel to give marine access. The swing bridge formerly stood across the entrance lock to South Dock and dates from 1855. It was moved here in 1986.

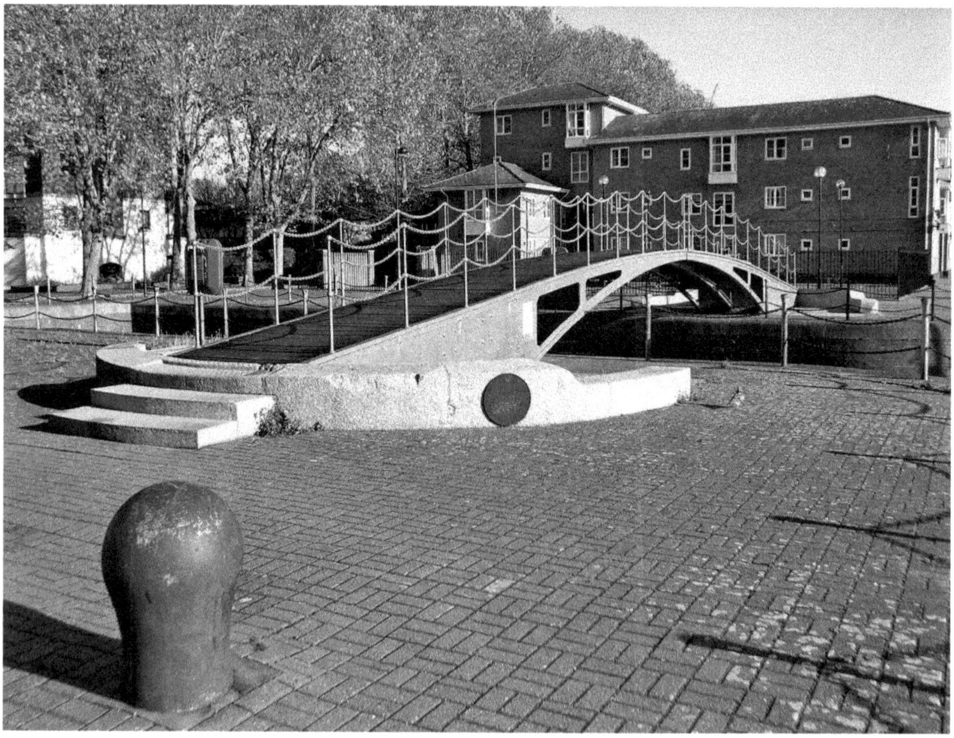

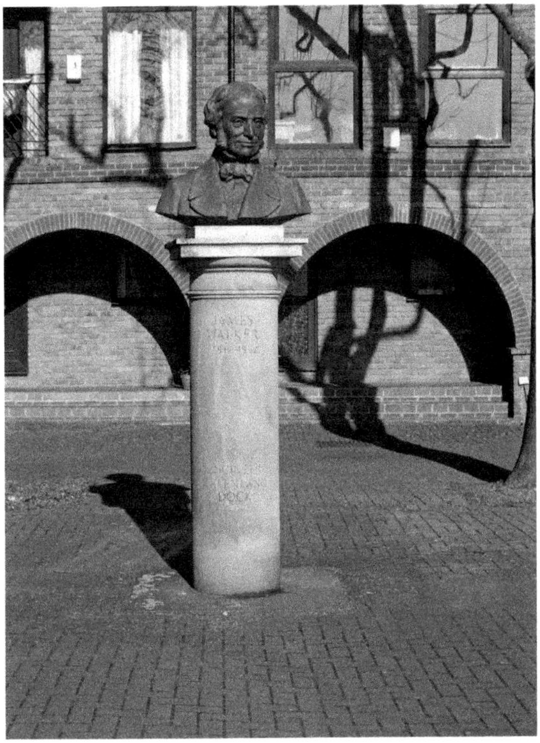

On display is this bust of James Walker (1781–1862). He rebuilt the dock between 1808 and 1810 and served as engineer of the Commercial Dock Company until his death. Among other things he was responsible for designing the swing bridge above.

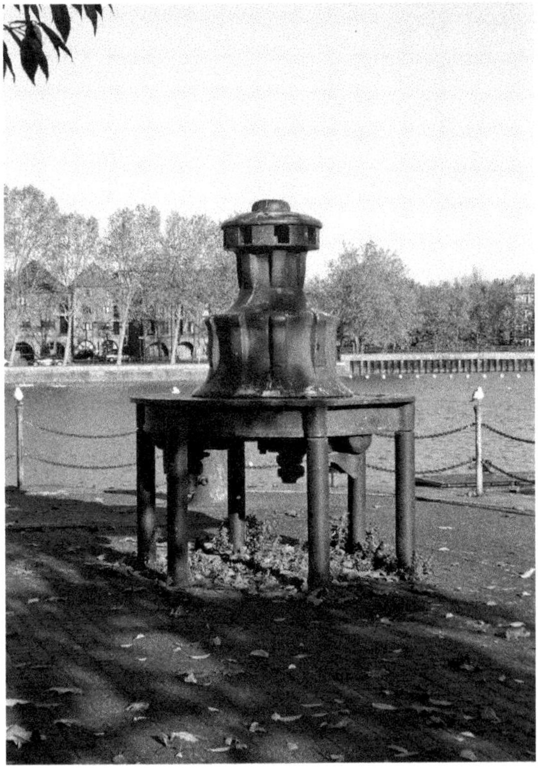

This capstan, a relic of former times, has been raised to display its machinery.

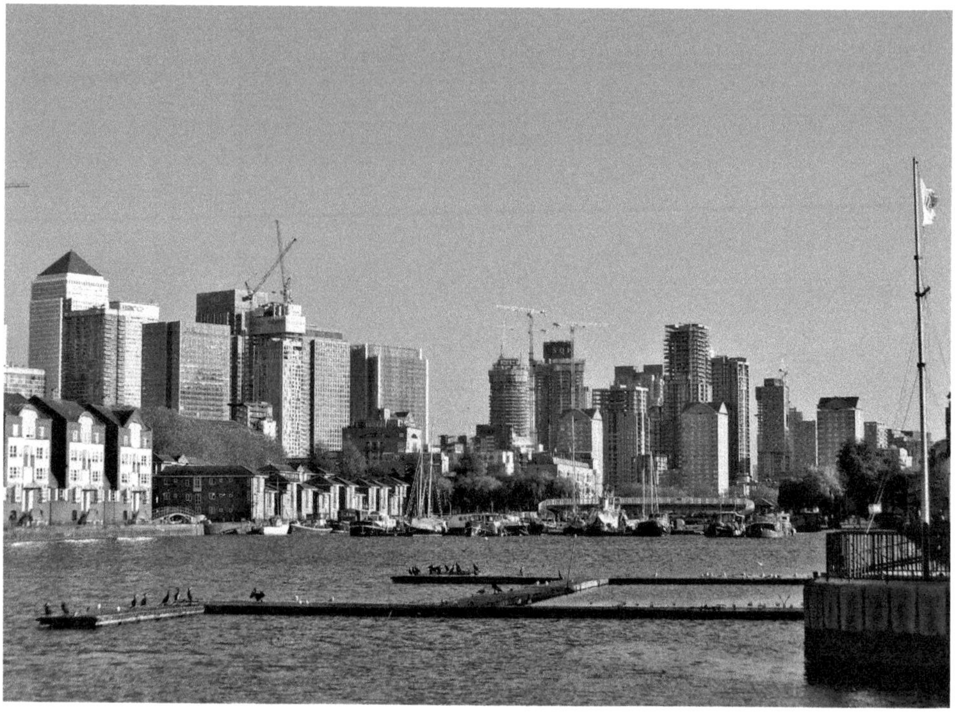

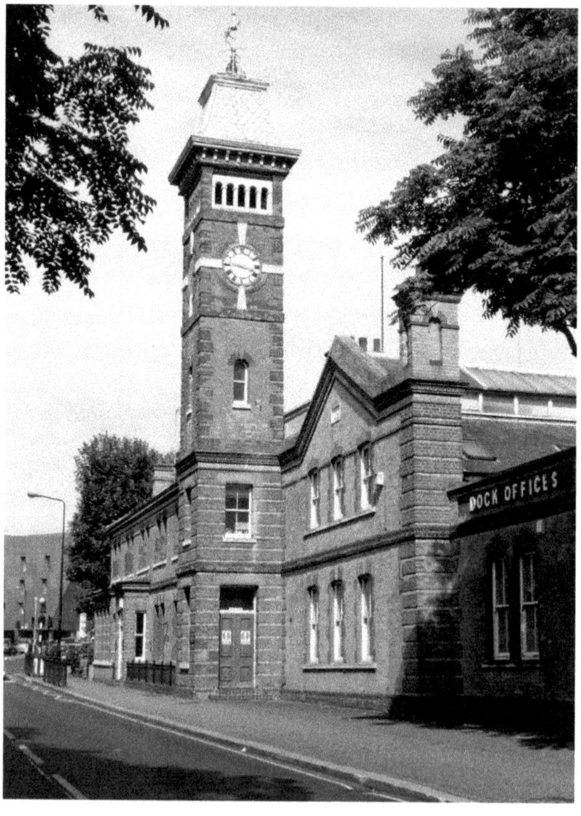

Above: Greenland Dock, marina and home to a watersports centre. The view is northwards to the vista of Canary Wharf on the opposite side of the Thames.

Left: Most prominent of the former buildings from the area's maritime days are the dock offices on Surrey Quays Road, the clock tower of which dominates the local scene.

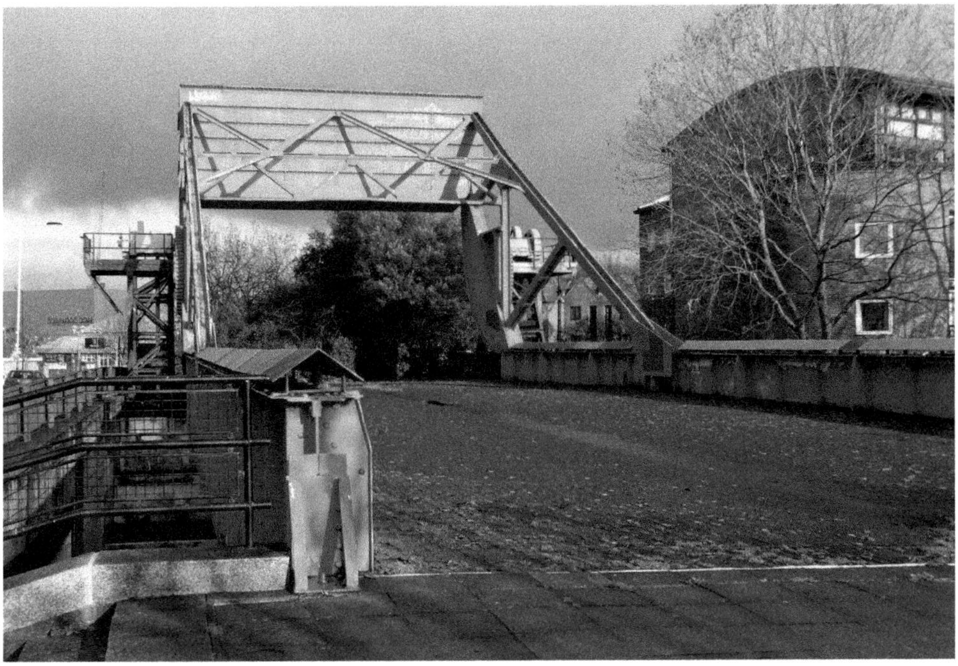

Redriff Road once crossed over this lifting bridge, but this is now disused and the road has been rerouted to the left of it.

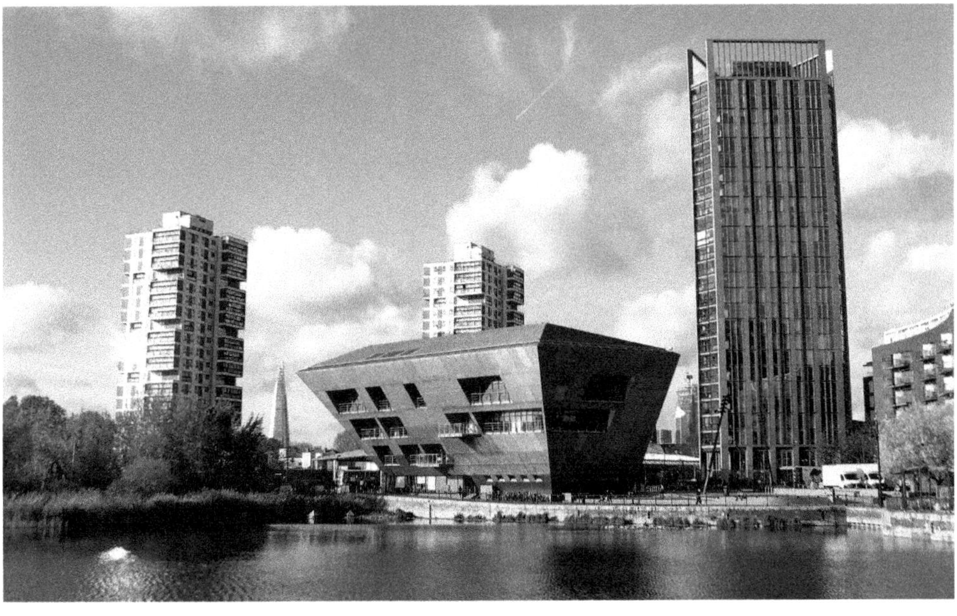

On the north side of Redriff Road is the Surrey Quays shopping centre with its car park. The nearby Surrey Docks station on the East London Line (now Overground) was renamed Surrey Quays when this opened in July 1988. Nearby is Canada Water with another station and bus station. The ziggurat-shaped building houses a library and theatre and was designed by architect Piers Gough. This opened in November 2011.

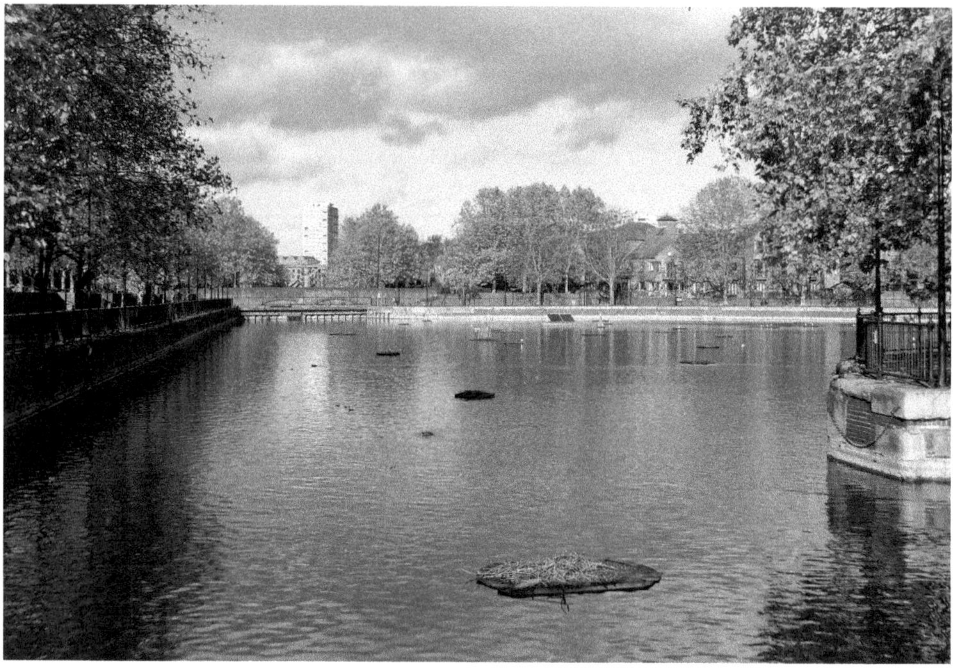

The various parts of the former Surrey Docks have suffered different fates, some being filled in. This is the quiet Surrey Water.

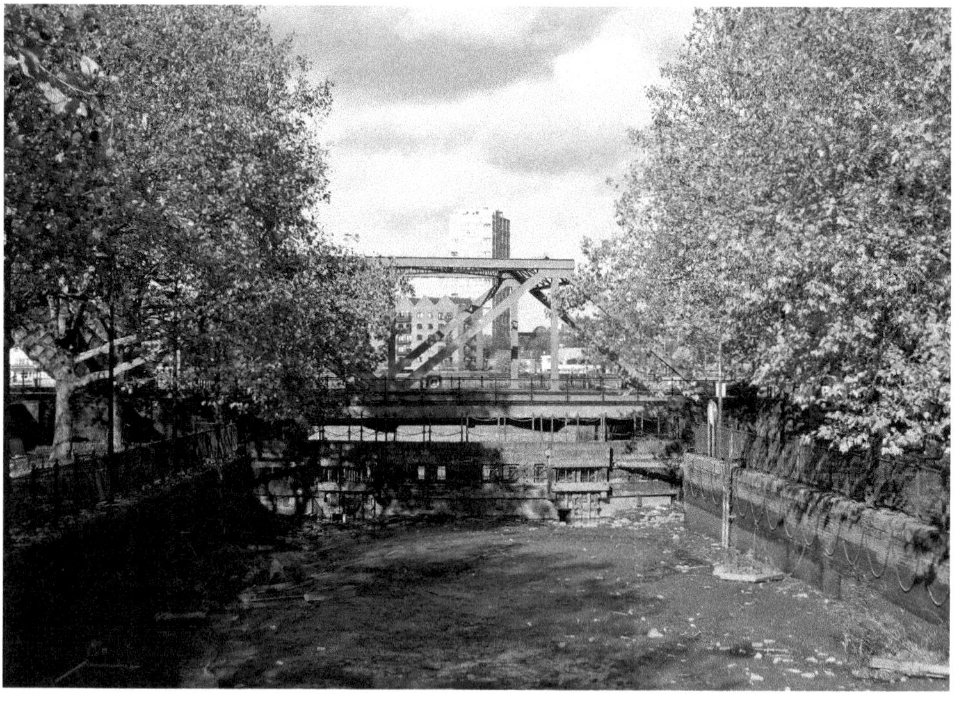

On Rotherhithe Street the entrance to Surrey Water was by a now disused lock that was crossed by a lifting bridge. This view is from Salter Road.

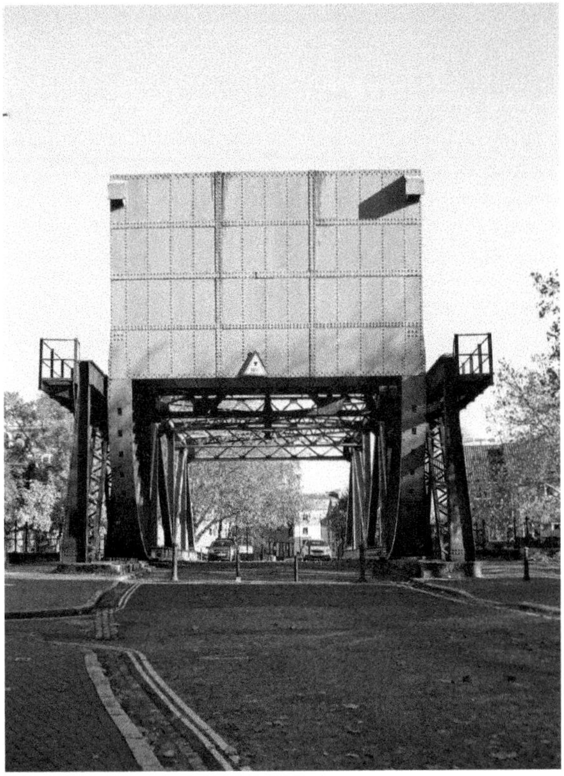

Right: A view of the now static lifting bridge on Rotherhithe Street.

Below: A former PLA pumphouse built in 1929 to regulate the water level in Surrey Docks is home to the Rotherhithe Heritage Museum and displays a collection of artefacts found on the Thames foreshore.

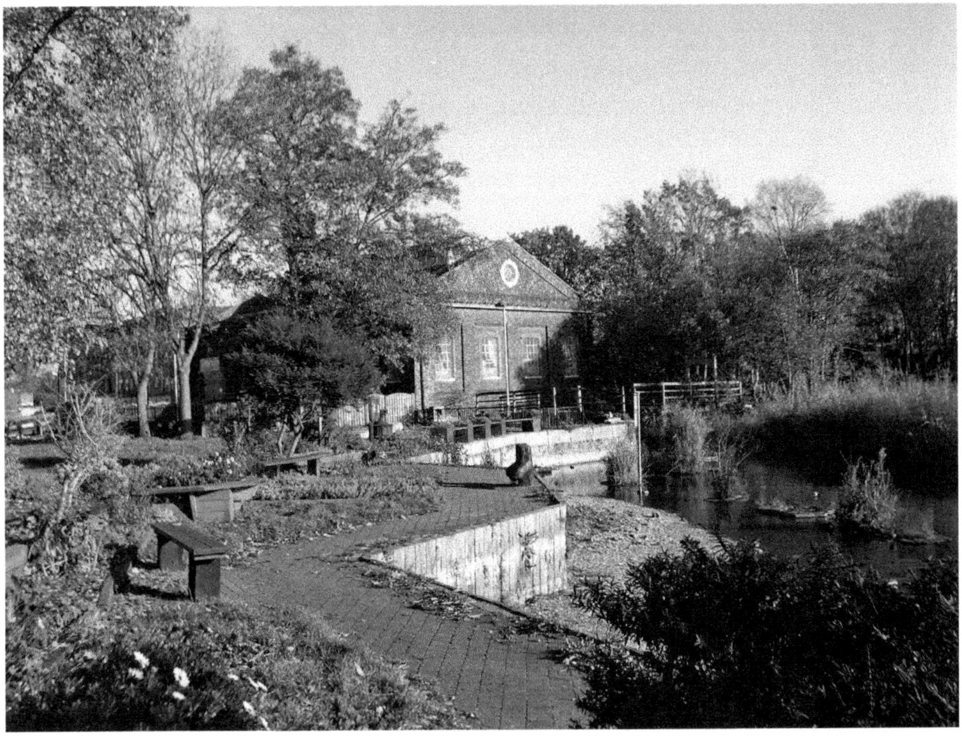

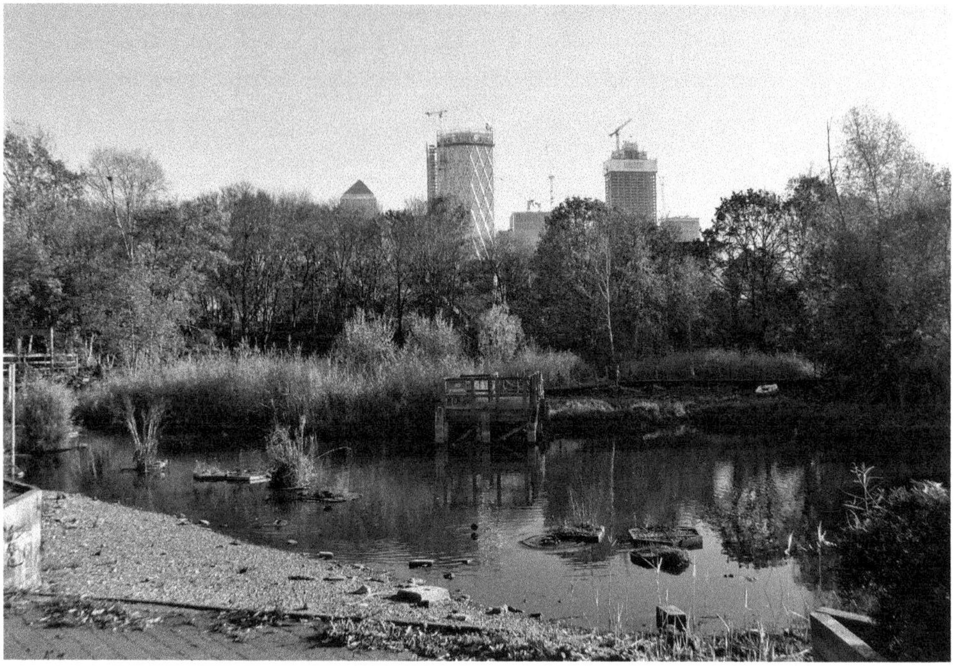

Next to the museum is Lavender Pond Nature Reserve, a man-made lake on the site of the old Lavender Dock.

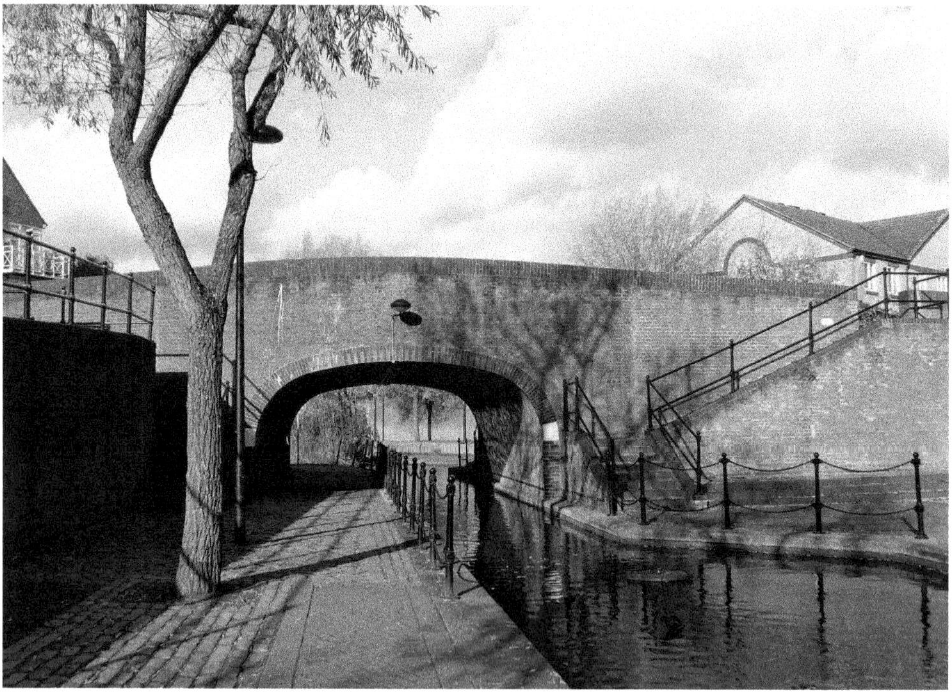

Parts of the former Surrey Docks were linked by waterways and a stretch has been retained that links Canada Water with Surrey Water, now incorporated into the housing development.

Deptford

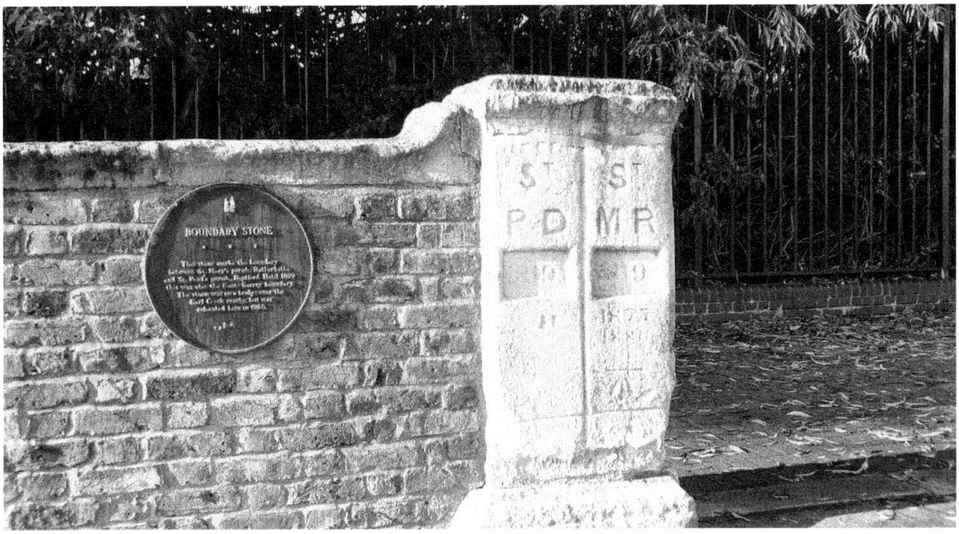

Continuing along the Thames Path beyond Greenland Pier into Deptford we encounter this boundary stone. It marks not only the boundary between Rotherhithe and Deptford parishes but also until 1899 the boundary between Surrey and Kent. The plaque states that the stone was formerly on a bridge over the Earl Creek, but was relocated here in 1988.

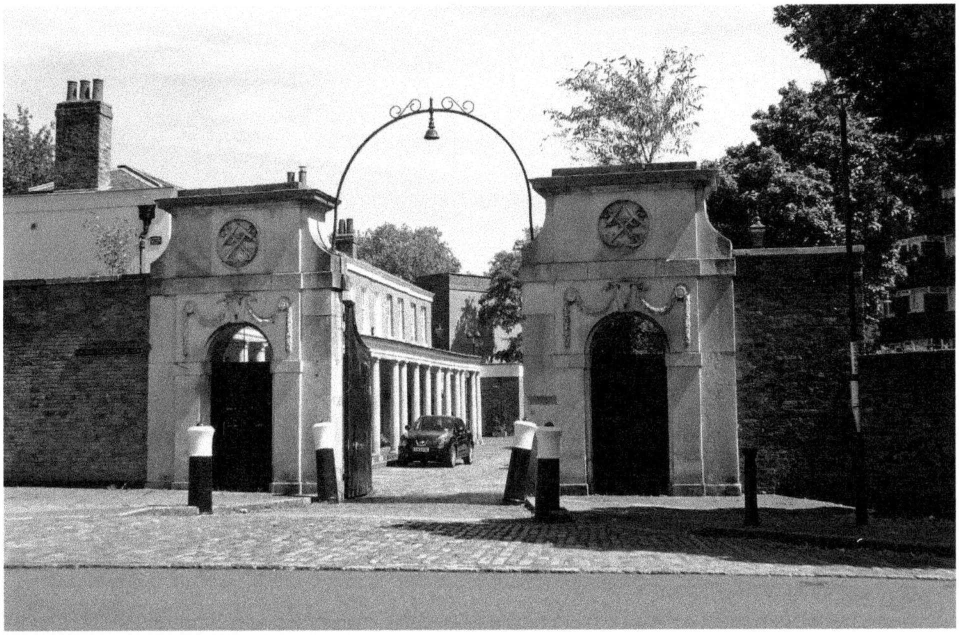

Deptford was the site of a royal dockyard from the sixteenth century. This was where the diarist Samuel Pepys worked in his capacity as Secretary of the Royal Navy. However, as ships got bigger and the site silted up, it became impractical and closed in 1869. This is the former entrance gates.

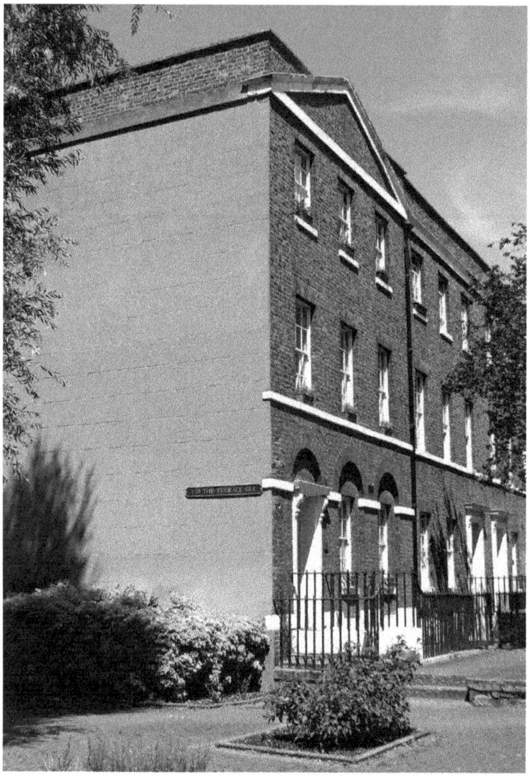

Left: A row of Georgian houses in The Terrace, SE8 – a reminder of the area's former importance.

Below: Part of the site was replaced by the Pepys Estate. This plaque announces that this was opened in July 1966 by Admiral of the Fleet, the Earl Mountbatten of Burma K.G.

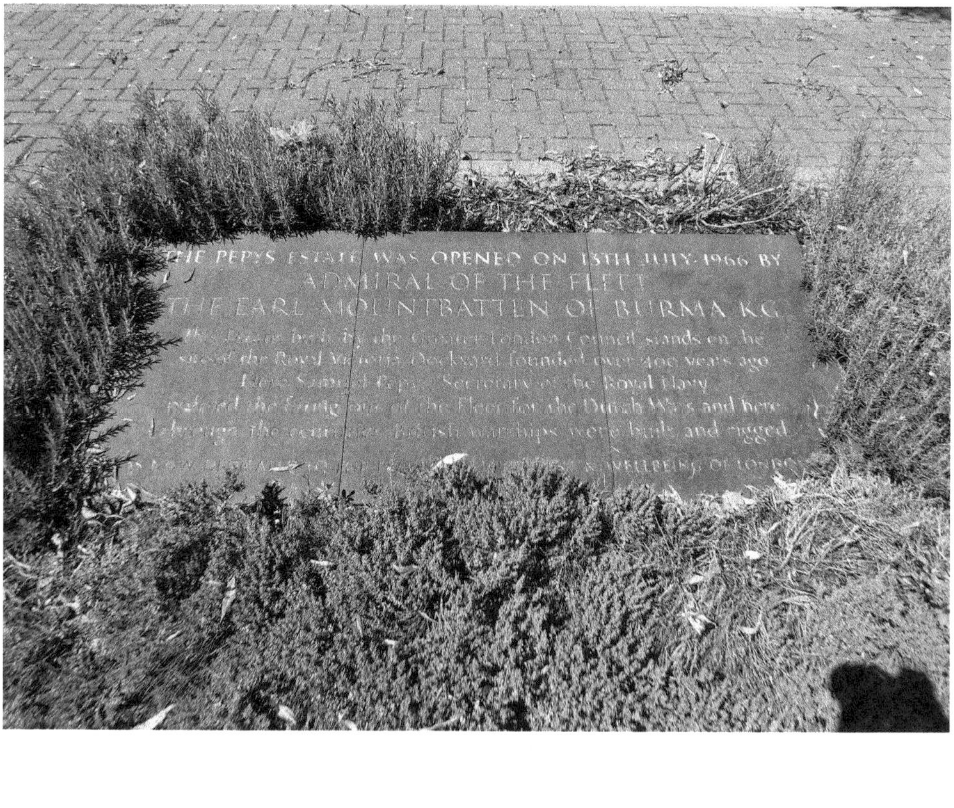

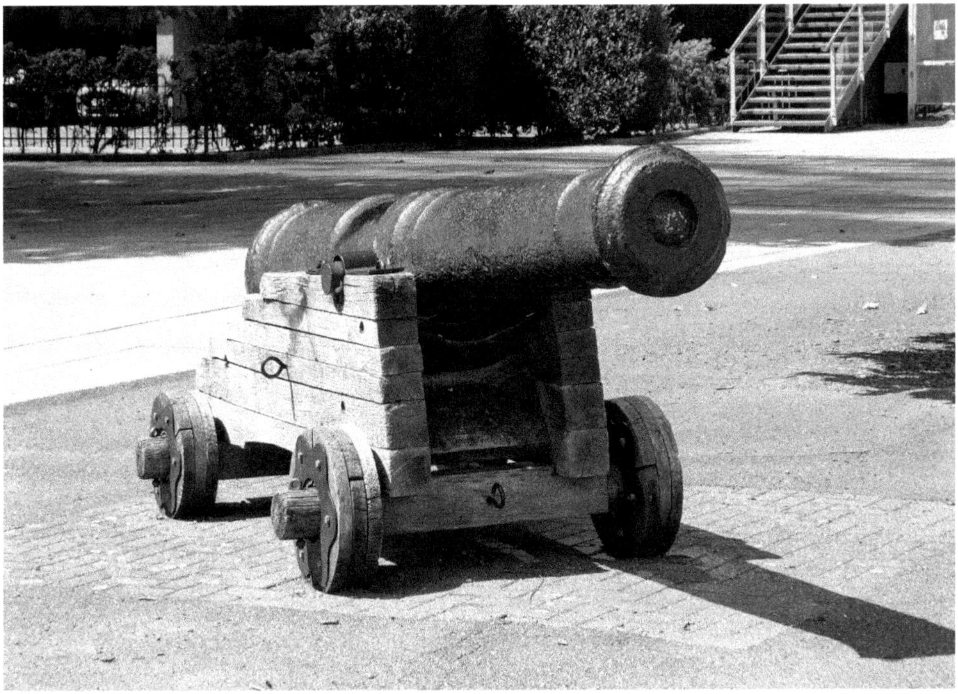

On the Deptford Strand foreshore, this old cannon is a reminder of the naval past.

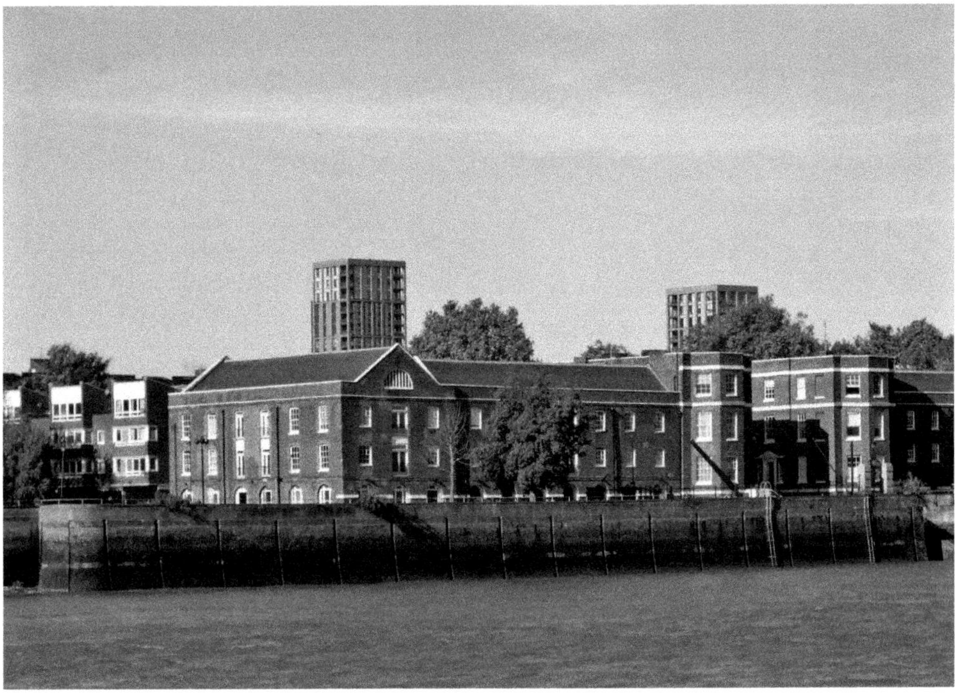

Two dark-brick buildings with arches along the lower storey remain. These are the remains of the Navy Victualling Yard, which was based here from 1788 to 1961.

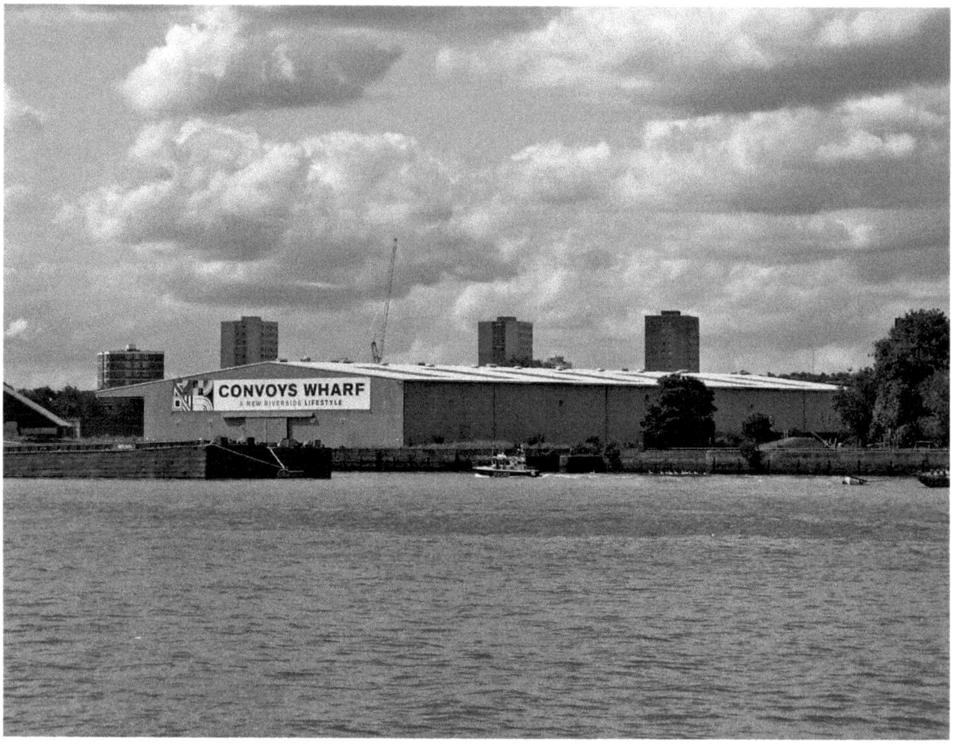

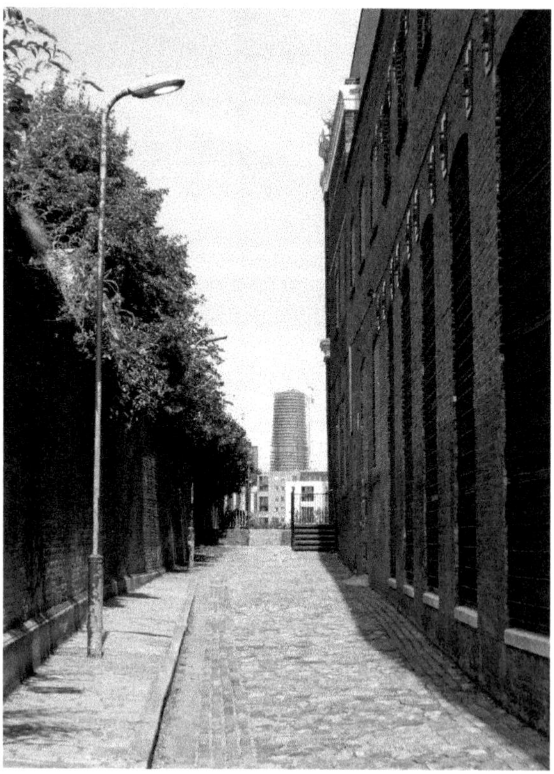

Above: A little further along is Convoys Wharf, where the industrial buildings await redevelopment almost inevitably for more housing. The Thames Path has to deviate inland around this complex.

Left: At various points along both sides of the river there were access points between buildings, where the public could reach the riverbank by stairs. This not only allowed for 'mudlarking', searching at low tide for objects washed up that could be sold, it was also where people could hire a boatman to cross the river or proceed along it. One such point now reopened is Watergate Street, Deptford. The modern tower block on the north bank rather spoils the period charm of the narrow cobbled way.

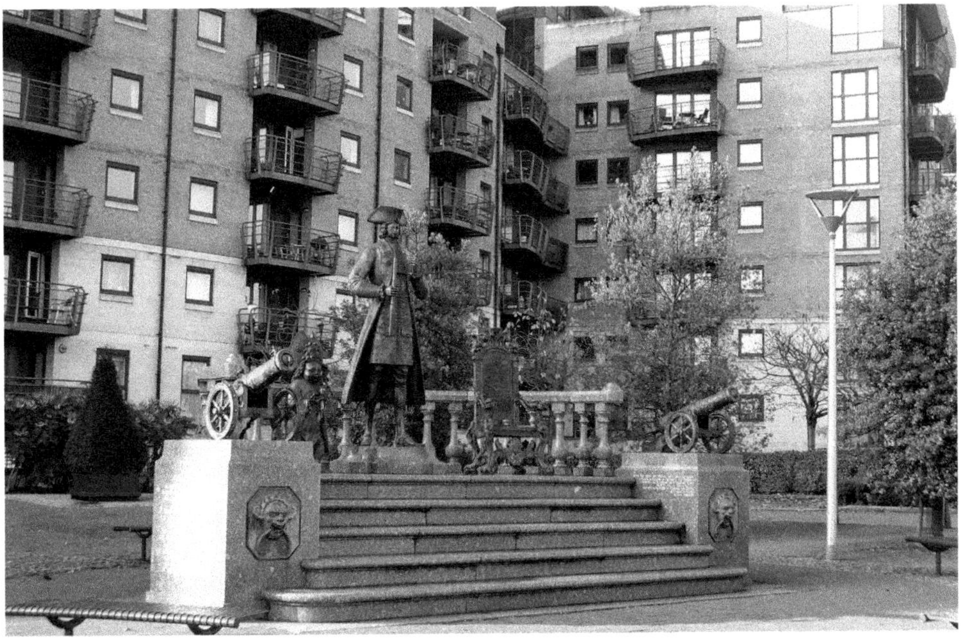

By the entrance to Deptford Creek is this statue of Peter the Great of Russia. In 1698, Peter came to England to study shipbuilding and rented the house of the writer John Evelyn in Deptford. The statue was erected in 1998, a gift from Russia to mark the tercentenary of his visit.

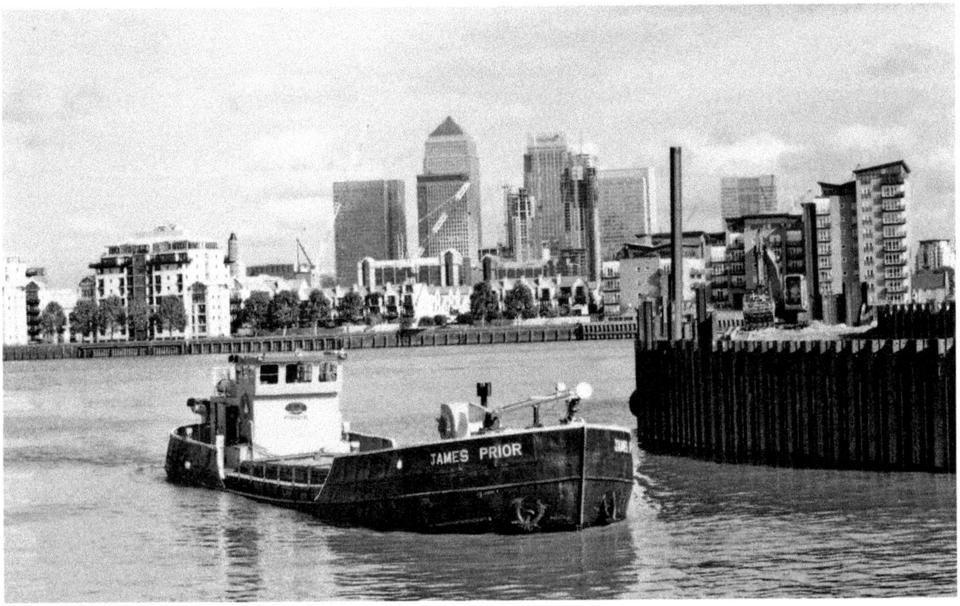

Deptford Creek is a tidal creek where the River Ravensbourne enters the Thames. Since 1870 the small vessels of J. J. Prior plied the Essex coast, and brought sand from their quarry at Fingringhoe on the River Colne near Wivenhoe up to London from 1933 until recently. *James Prior* (1963, 300 tons) is turning into the Creek on 25 September 2007. The towers of Canary Wharf are prominent on the other bank.

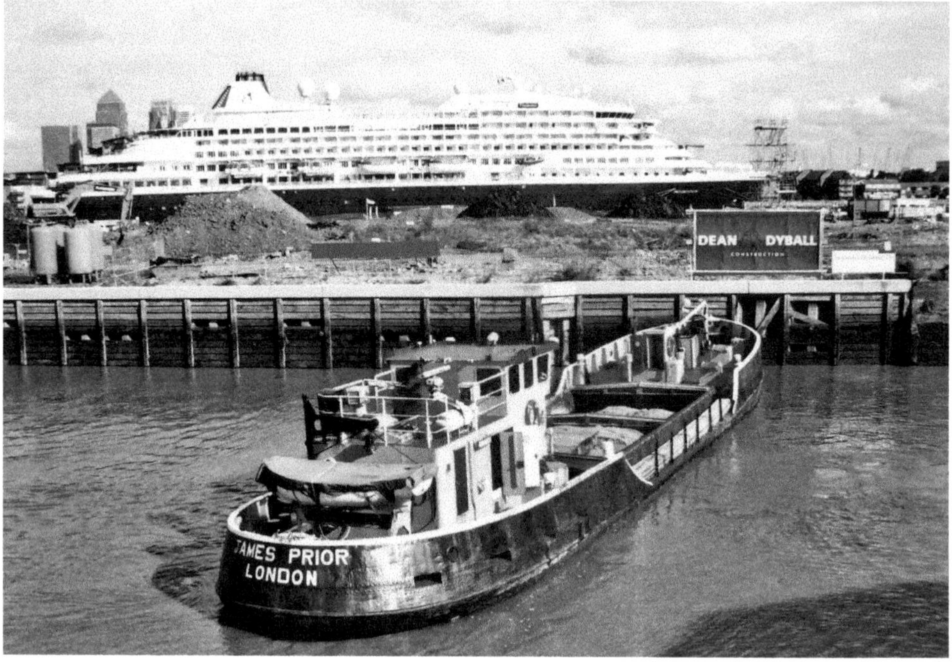

James Prior turns in Deptford Creek on 25 September 2007. A cruise ship, the *Prinsendam,* is anchored on Greenwich Tier.

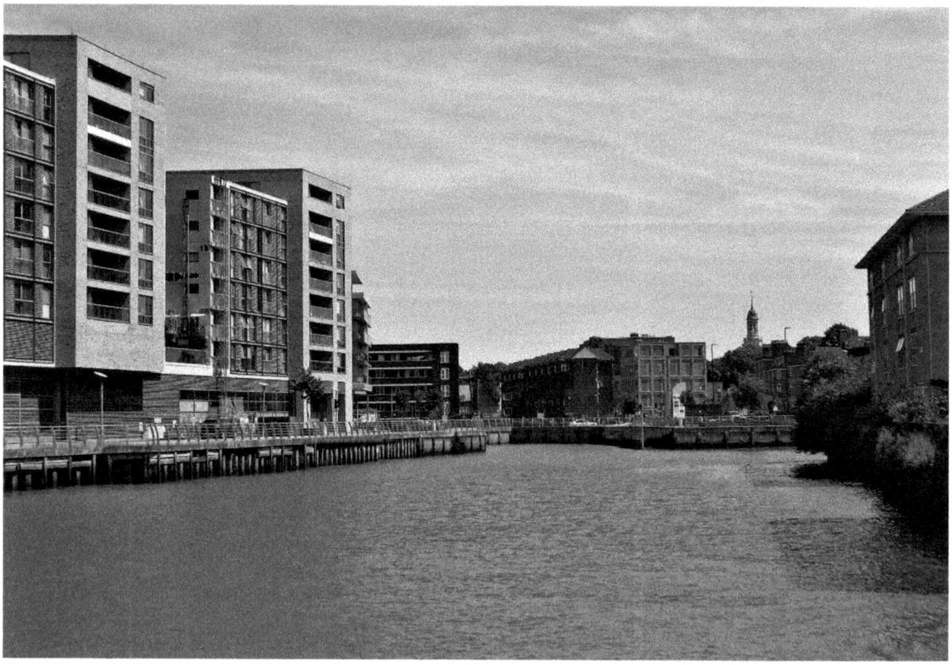

Since the previous photograph was taken the building work seen being started has been completed and Deptford Creek has been transformed with new housing. This view from mid-2020 is looking back towards Greenwich with the parish church of St Alfege in the distance.

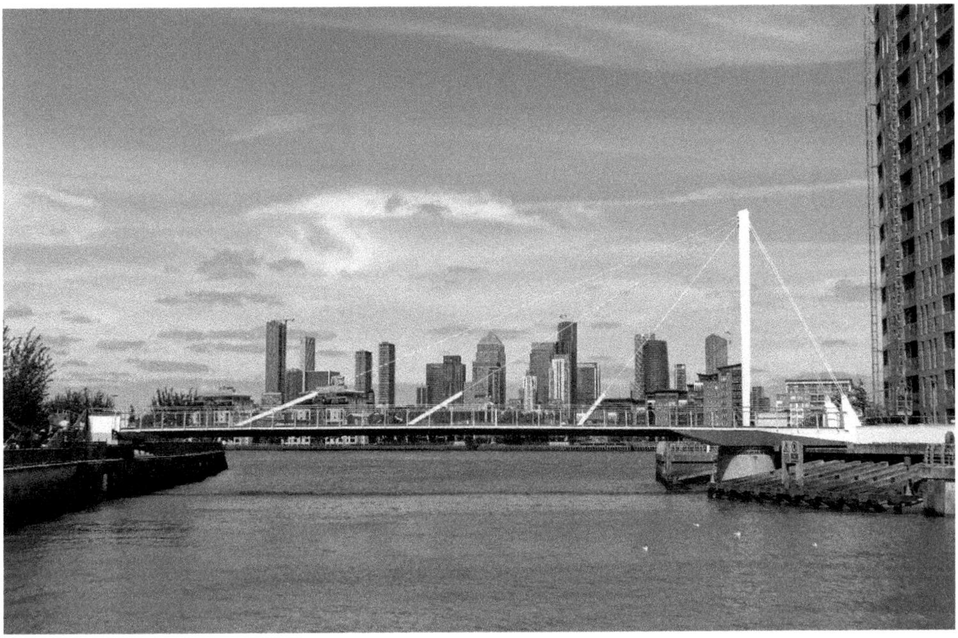

At the entrance to Deptford Creek where we saw *James Prior* turning in, a new swivelling footbridge has been installed to link the new housing developments to the Thames Path riverbank.

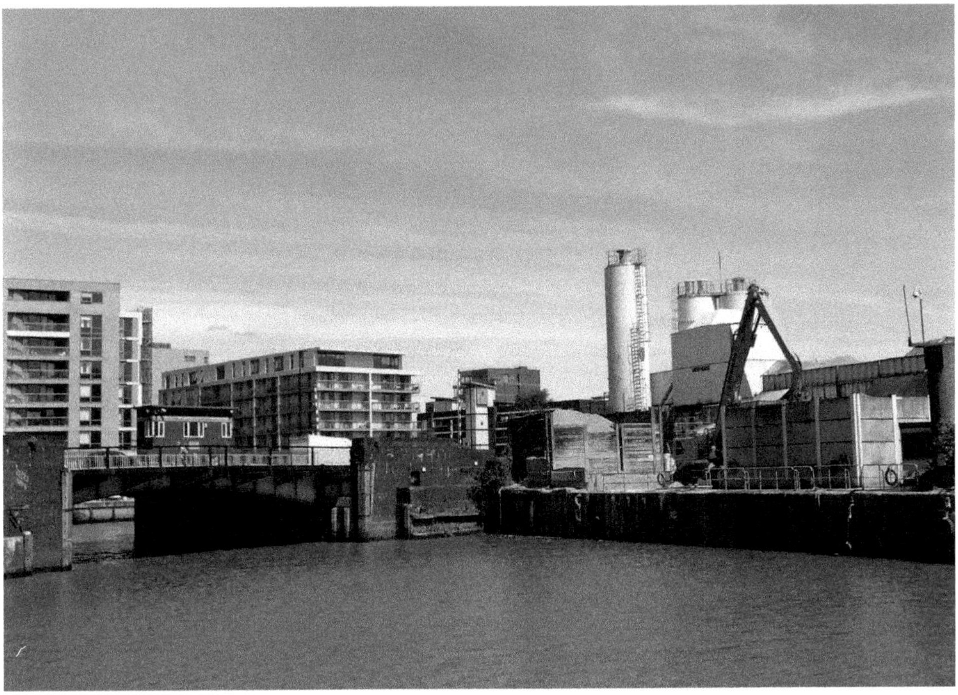

The wharf where the sand barges used to unload is directly south of the road bridge on Creek Road.

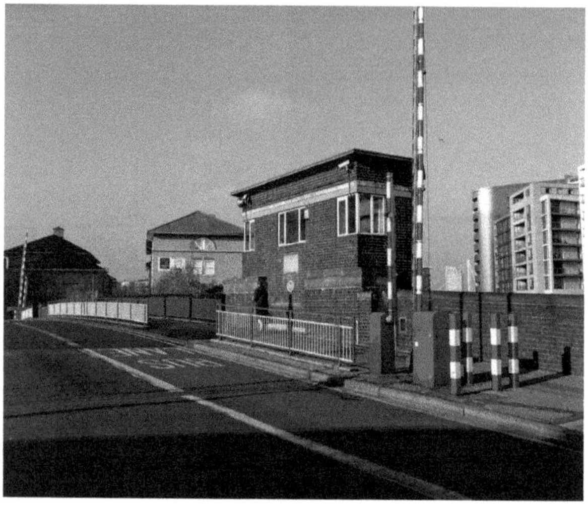

To allow vessels to access the Creek there is a lifting bridge on Creek Road, controlled from the building seen here.

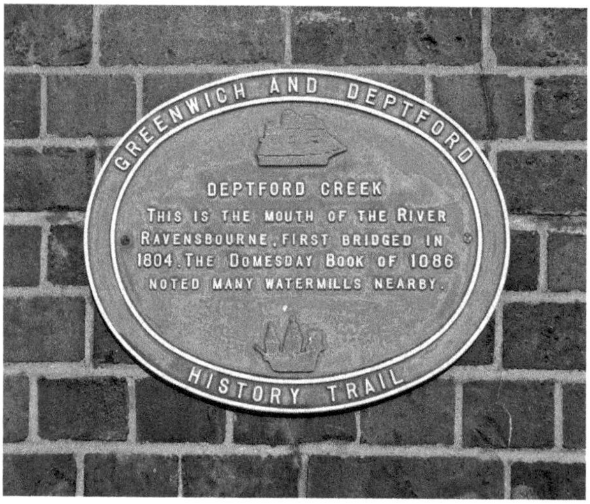

A plaque erected by the Greenwich and Deptford History Trail adorns the side of the bridge control building.

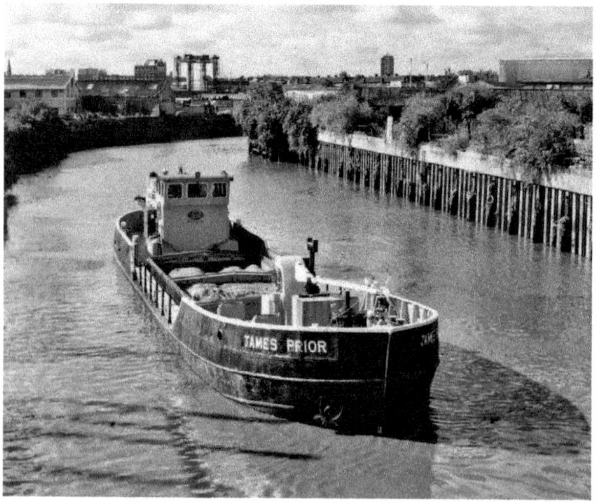

Deptford Creek looking south from Creek Road in September 2007 with *James Prior* again. The four-legged structure visible in the distance is the lifting span of the railway bridge that crosses the Creek.

To Greenwich Pier

Our journey ends at Greenwich Pier, terminus for many of the tourist boats that travel down river from Tower Pier. Greenwich has many attractions and is patronised by thousands of tourists. These will be examined in the companion volume, which will continue along the Thames Path and Thames Path Extension to Woolwich and beyond. Some tourist boats continue to the O2 Arena and the Thames Clipper commuter ferries continue as far as Woolwich at certain times.

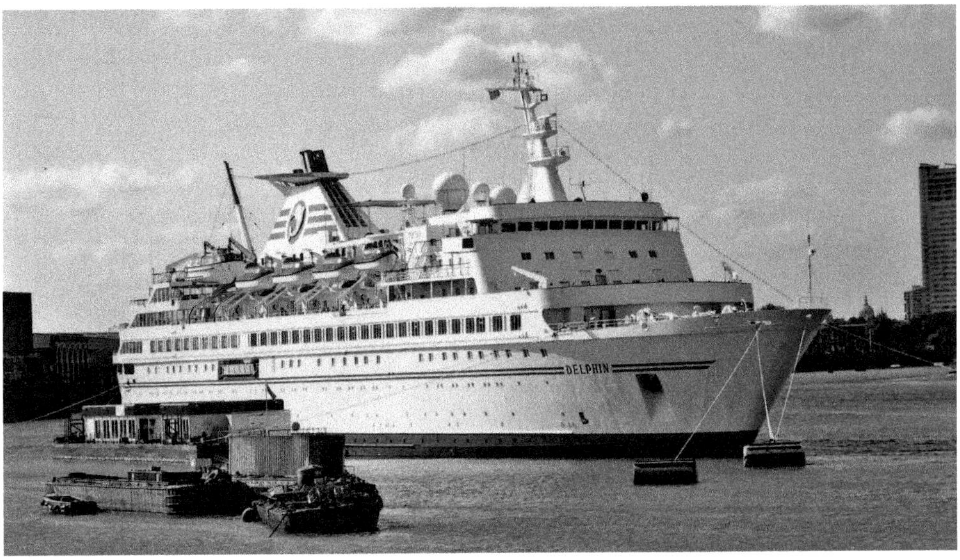

Cruise ships visiting London sometimes come upriver and moor at Greenwich Tier, just beyond the pier. This is the *Delphin*, visiting in September 2006.

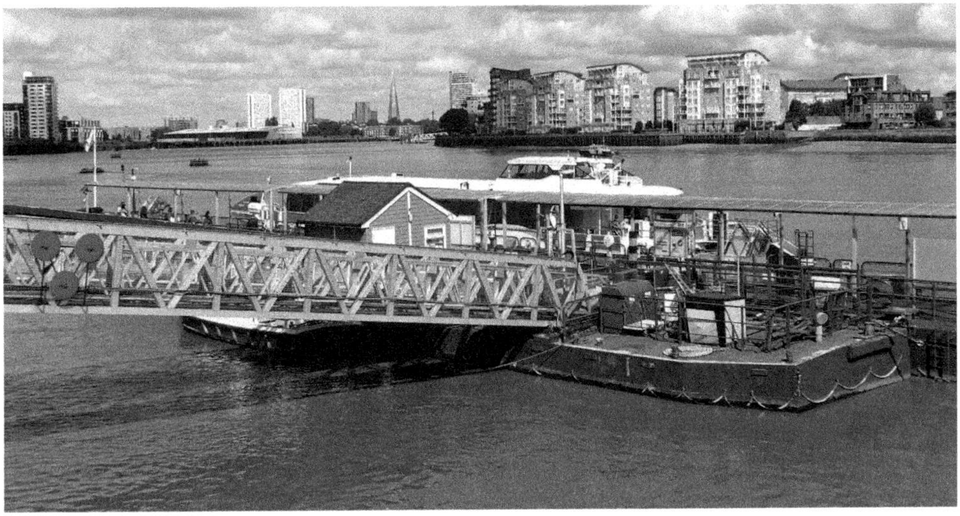

Greenwich Pier in 2020, with one of the frequent Thames Clipper ferries paying a call.

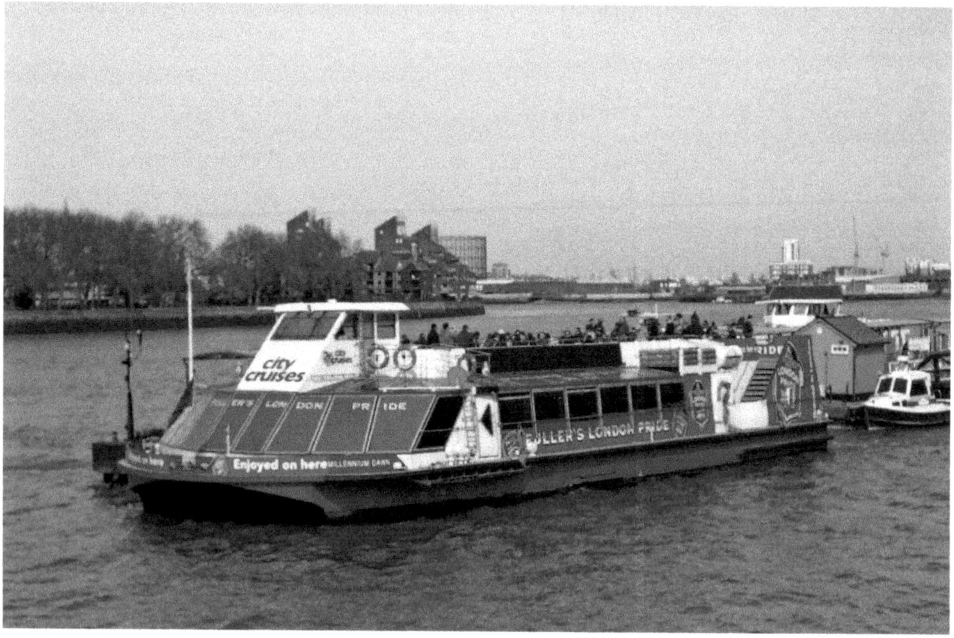

A well-laden vessel of City Cruises, one of the 'Millennium class' catamarans *Millennium Dawn* takes on passengers in April 2013. The pier was upgraded in the early 2000s with disabled access and new ticketing and catering facilities.

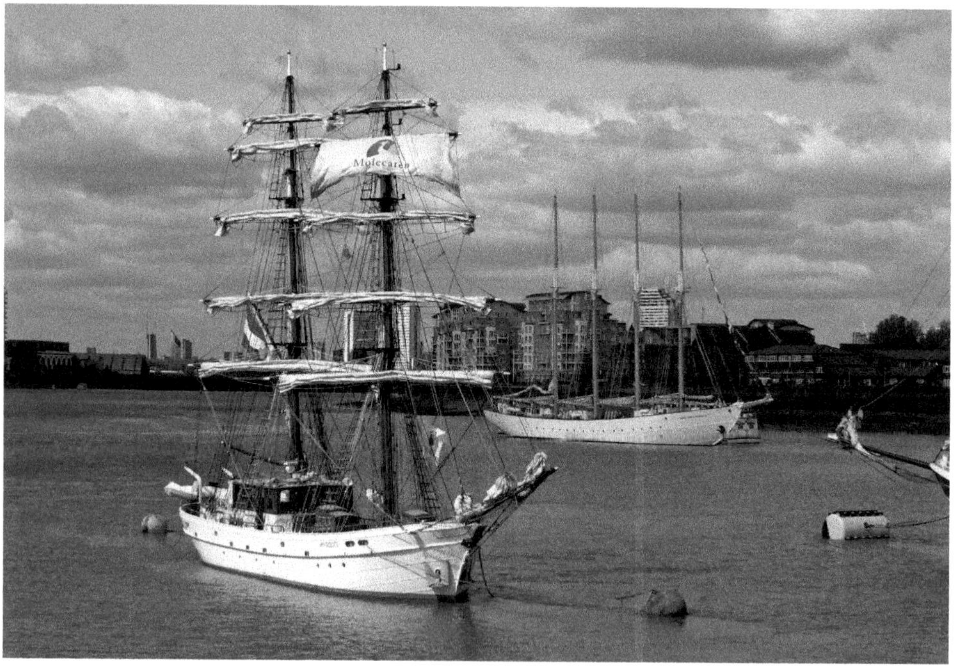

The Rendez-Vous 2017 Tall Ships Regatta started from Greenwich in April 2017 and brought a wide variety of sailing ships to the river. These two are the *Aphodite* (nearest) and the *Santa Maria Manuela,* which was constructed in 1937. Taken on 16 April 2017.

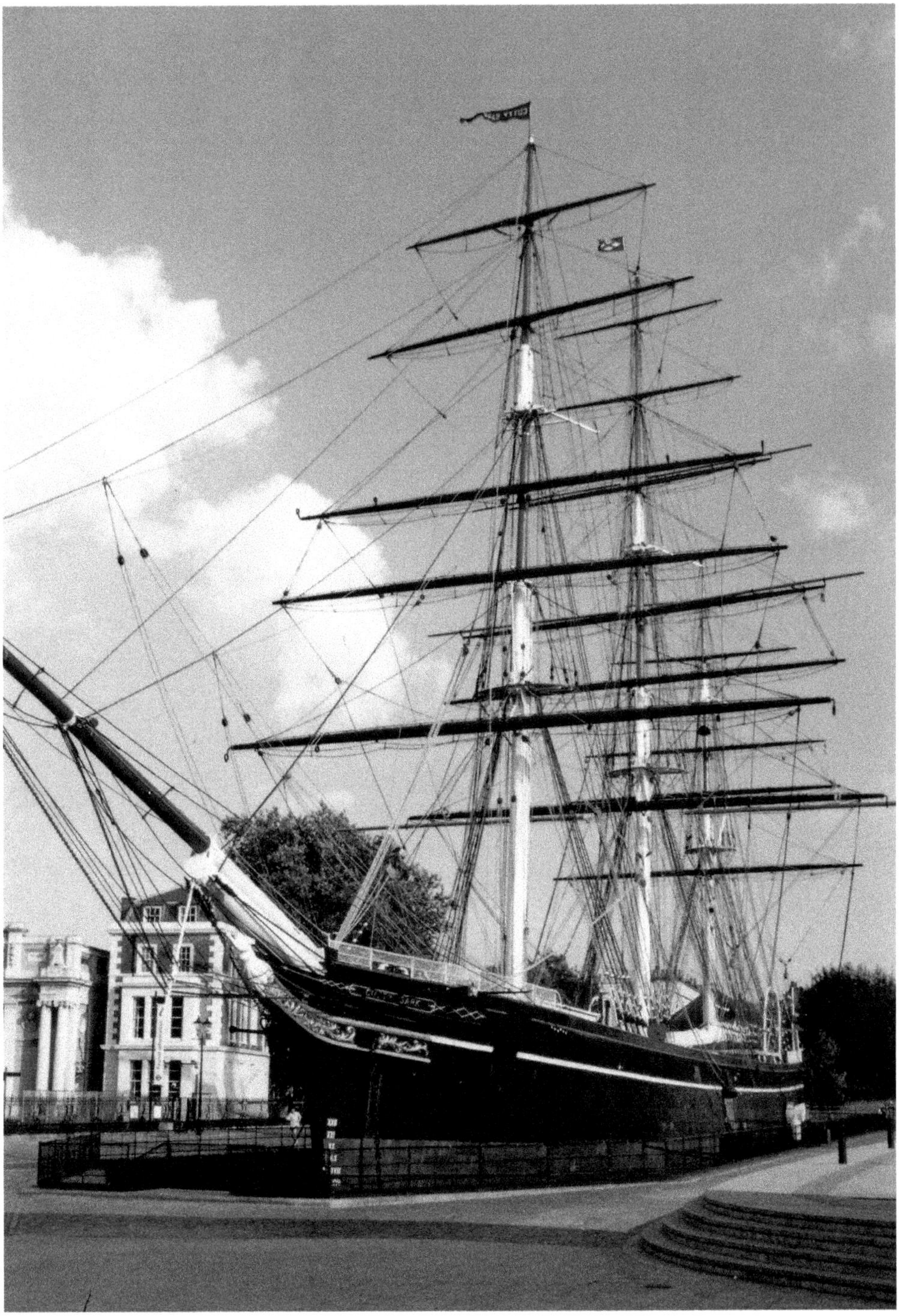

There can be few ships more famous than the *Cutty Sark*. Built as a tea clipper in 1869 and later employed in the wool trade from Australia, she survived by virtue of later being used as a static training ship. She arrived at Greenwich for preservation in a dry dock in 1954. This view shows how the vessel used to look prior to 2007.

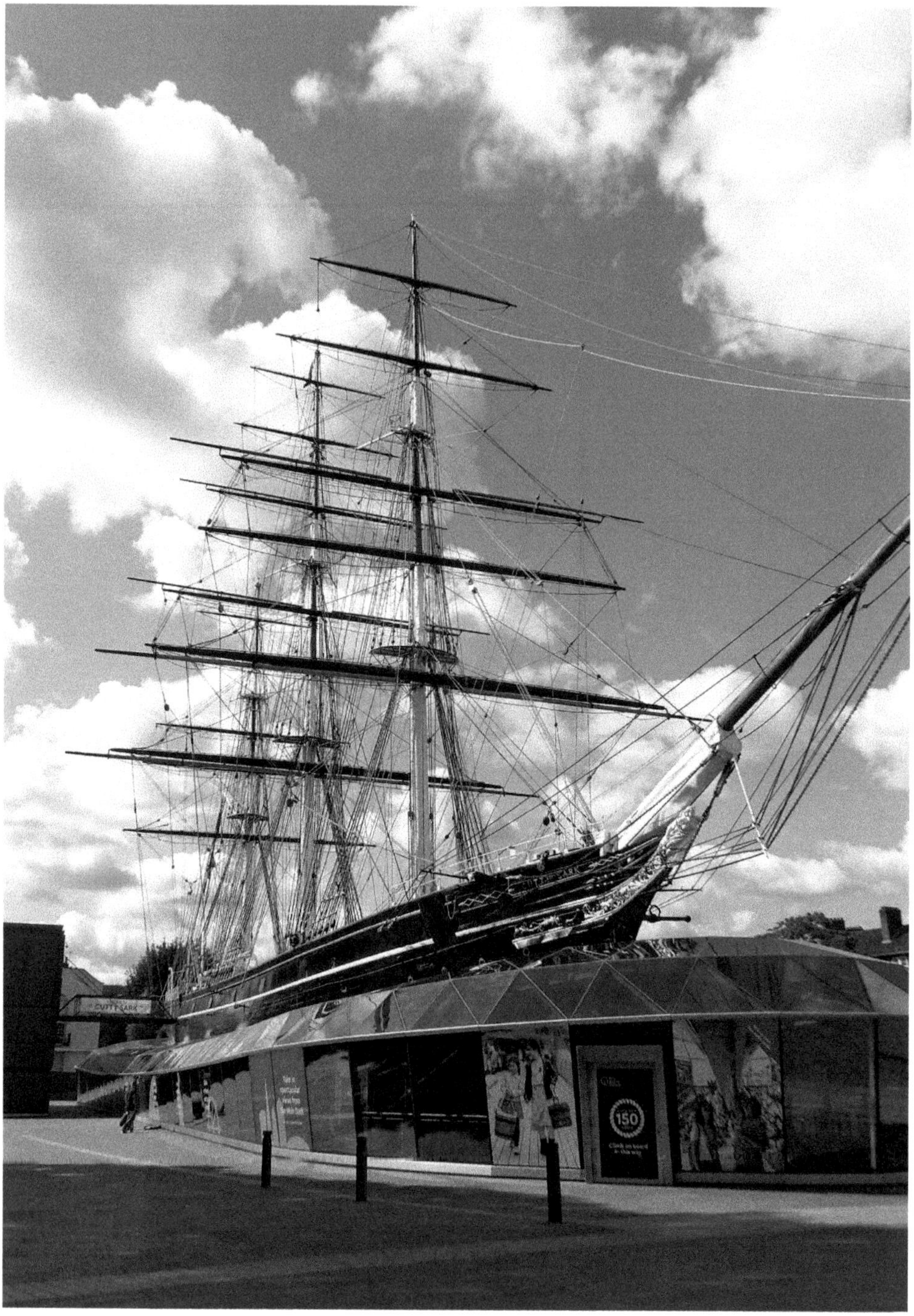

Disaster struck during renovation when a fire broke out on 21 May 2007, apparently caused by an industrial vacuum cleaner left running throughout the weekend. Although there was extensive damage much of the timber had been removed from the ship for restoration and so was not affected. The renovation has seen the ship now raised on steel props so that visitors can pass underneath her hull, which is now controversially enclosed.

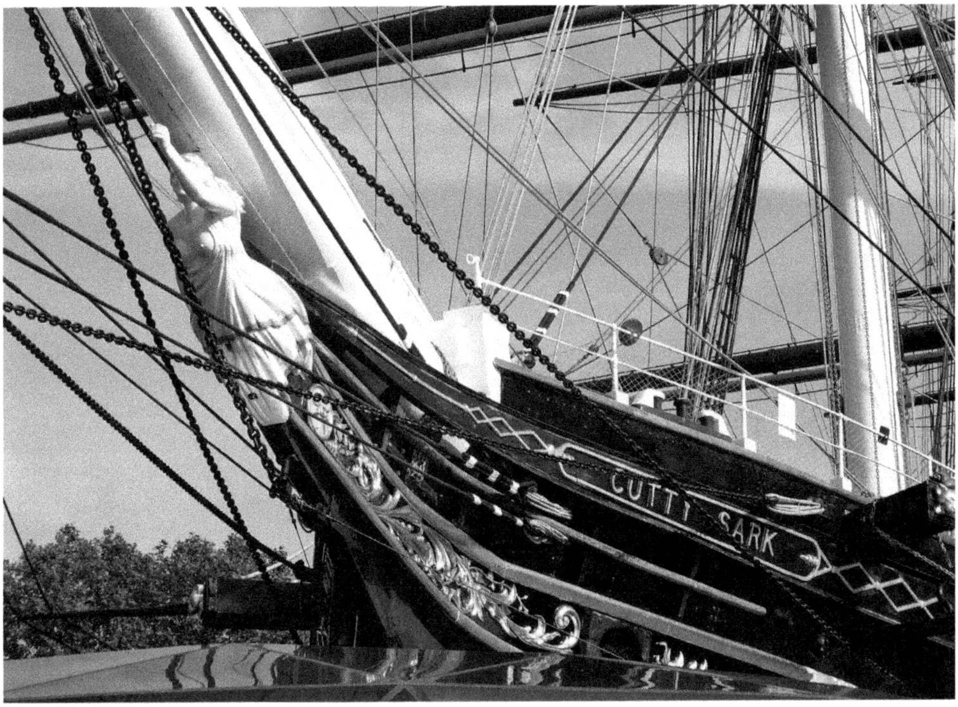

The current figurehead of the *Cutty Sark*. The name derives from the nickname given to the witch Nannie Dee in Robert Burns poem 'Tam o' Shanter' and means the short shirt or chemise she was wearing.

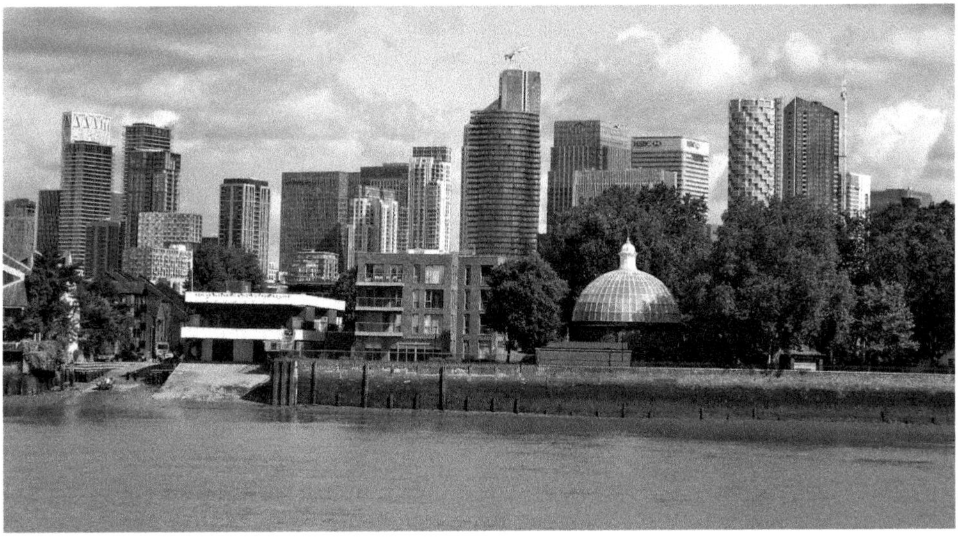

The view from south to north bank at Greenwich could not be more different than that from north to south (see p. 59). The skyline is dominated by the towers of the Canary Wharf financial quarter. The domed building among the trees of Island Gardens park is the access to the foot tunnel under the river. To the left the building with the slipway in front is the premises of the Poplar, Blackwall & District Rowing Club.

Acknowledgements and Bibliography

Cameron-Cooper, Gilly, *Walking London's Docks, Rivers & Canals* (London, New Holland, 2005)
Clapham, Phoebe, *Thames Path in London* (London, Aurum, 2018)
Clegg, W. Paul, *Docks and Ports:2 London* (Shepperton, Ian Allan, 1987)
Lunn, Geoff, *Port of London Through Time* (Stroud, Amberley, 2011)
McNeil, Ian, *Hydraulic Power* (London, Longman, 1972)
London A-Z (Borough Green, Geographers' A-Z Map Company Ltd, edition 10, 2012)

Museum of London Docklands
www.museumoflondon.org.uk

Brunel Museum, Rotherhithe
www.thebrunelmuseum.com

Exploring East London: An excellent website with maps, created by the late Lawrence Rigal, who died in 2010. Although no longer being updated, the website remains available and is an ideal source for anyone wanting to explore the area, although some of the featured locations have closed, or been lost to redevelopment.
www.exploringeastlondon.co.uk

Thames Path
www.thames-path.org.uk

Transport for London: Divided into for four sections north and south banks in the Greater London area with useful walking tour maps and informative text.
www.tfl.gov.uk/modes/walking/thames-path

All photographs are by the author except where credited.